S0-ATF-912

Sami Rahman

Getting Started: iPads for Special Needs

Edition 1

Getting Started: iPads for Special Needs, 1st Edition
Published by:
Rahman Publishing
Houston, Texas
www.ipads4specialneedsbook.com

All rights reserved. No part of this book may be used or reproduced by any means, graphic, electronic, or mechanical, including photocopying, recording, taping or by any information storage retrieval system without the written permission of the publisher except in the case of brief quotations embodied in critical articles and reviews. The views expressed in this work are solely those of the author. Because of the dynamic nature of the Internet, any Web addresses or links contained in this book may have changed since publication and may no longer be valid.

Apple®, FaceTime®, iCal®, iMessage™, iMovie®, iPad®, iPhone®, iPhoto®, iPod®, iPod touch®, iTunes®, iTunes U®, Keynote®, Mac®, Safari®, App StoreSM, Apple Store®, Genius®, iCloud®, iTunes Store®, and MobileMe® are trademarks of Apple Inc., registered in the U.S. and other countries.

The Bluetooth® word mark and logos are registered trademarks owned by Bluetooth SIG, Inc.

IOS® is a trademark or registered trademark of Cisco in the U.S. and other countries.

YouTube® and Android ™ are registered trademarks of Google, Inc.

Any and all other trademarked products and terms mentioned herein are the registered trademarks of their respective owners and no infringement of those trademarks is intended.

ISBN 13: 978-0-9851680-0-1

Copyright © 2012 by Sami Rahman

For Noah, my hero, you work so hard! I can only hope to keep up.

Love Dad

Authors Acknowledgements

I would like to thank my wife Laura for helping me in so many ways to make this book possible, the editing (yes, she even edited this line), the encouragement, and all of the love I feel every day. I would like to thank my dad, Badia Rahman, for taking so many great pictures and his energy and time. I would like to thank Cristen Reat, co-founder of BridgingApps.org, for her friendship, her insight and encouragement, and the team of great people at Easter Seals of Greater Houston, where BridgingApps has found a home and is flourishing beyond our wildest dream.

Lastly, I would like to thank Noah's therapists and teachers who have poured their love, hopes, and desires into him as if he were their own child. Laura, Noah, Maya and I are so grateful for their support. It is so amazing to me that it brings tears to my eyes. In a good way.

We what to hear from you?

Your feedback is very important to us. If you have any comments or feedback, positive or otherwise we want to hear from you. Please contact us via our website:

http://www.ipads4specialneedsbook.com

Thank you in advance.

If you need more help with your iPad you can contact me via BridgingApps. org, a program of Easter Seals of Greater Houston.

http://www.bridgingapps.org

Table Of Contents

CHAPTER

Introduction

Why I wrote this book and who is it for?

About the Author

My name is Sami Rahman. My wife Laura and I are the parents of 2 children, a boy named Noah who is 4 and a girl, Maya age 2 (at the time of this writing). We live in Houston, Texas. Noah has Cerebral Palsy as well as a condition known as Short Gut Syndrome. Professionally, I run a technology company, so I am very comfortable around computers.

As I got more involved with the iPad, I began attending meetings with a group of parents to share use, apps and advice all centered around the iPad®. The group was originally called iPads for Parents, and was started by Cristen Reat in October 2010. In November 2010, I started a website named Special Needs Apps for Kids (*SNApps4Kids.com*). The goal was to create a website where we could capture the information we were exchanging in our group meetings and make that information accessible to a larger audience. In May of 2011, we decided to merge our efforts with Easter Seals of Greater Houston. Easter Seals is the largest service provider to the special needs community in North America, so it was a natural fit. It has been a great partnership.

As *SNApps4Kids.com* started to really take off, it became clear to us that we really need to better understand the world of assistive technology and be able to speak to a much broader audience, so in the summer of 2011, Cristen and I took a Assistive Technology Applications Certification Program offered by California State University. This course, the people I met, and the things I learned have had such an enormous impact on how I think, how I problem solve, how I approach every new challenge when it comes to the iPad, and how I respond to the various issues we are presented with at *SNApps4Kids.com*. In 2012, *SNApps4Kids.com* became *BrigdingApps.org*™ - same mission, different name.

Our Story - Noah

In April 2008, our son Noah was born 13 weeks prematurely. As a result of his extreme prematurity, Noah has two major issues. First, during our 6 month stay at the NICU (neonatal intensive care unit), he developed NEC (necrotizing entercolitis), which is an infection in the intestines. As a result of the infection, 70% of his small intestines and 50% of his large intestines were removed. Since this illness left Noah with essentially the bare minimum tools for nutrition and water intake for the body, his nutritional needs are a very large part of our focus. The resulting condition is known as Short Gut Syndrome, and, frankly, we still can't believe it is even possible to survive with so much of his digestive tract removed, let alone thrive. But, as you undoubtably know, there are many things about special needs kids that go beyond the normal realm of belief and viability. My son is my hero.

The second major concern is that he has moderate Cerebral Palsy resulting from trauma at birth. Cerebral Palsy is an umbrella term for brain damage that can affect the neurological pathways between the brain and the body. Noah has a number of muscles that are always flexed, that is, having high tone (spasticity) and others that are always more relaxed, that exhibit low tone. In other words, muscle-wise, his body is always out of balance. The struggle is to create muscle balance through therapy, stretching, drugs, or other interventions while he is still growing, all the while knowing that with each growth spurt he has, a new imbalance is created. As of this writing, Noah can crawl on all fours, but does not walk without using a walker (gait trainer). He also has a manual wheel chair.

In May 2010, when he was 2 years old, Noah was assessed as being 12 months behind cognitively and in the area of language development. At the same time, his Early Childhood Intervention coordinator suggested that Noah might benefit from an iPad. As a technology guy, I figured this was a great excuse to buy some new tech, and if he did not like it, I would get a new iPad out of it. Good for him if he liked it; good for me if he didn't. Well, here is the thing - four months later, we did another assessment, and he was now essentially on par in both cognitive and language development skills. In four very short months, he developed 12 months worth of cognitive and language skills! I am not going to tell you that the iPad is a magic bullet, though, or that every child who uses it will have the same amazing results. What I will say is that with a lot of hard work, and the right kind of intervention and therapy, the results can be much more than you ever hoped.

When we first started, Noah would lick the screen until we had to intervene, and I would think to myself, "that ain't right, how educational can licking the screen be?" And, truthfully, I still see him doing it now every once in a while and think the same thing. But when we started, it was all about getting him interested in the iPad. Once we did that, delivering new experiences - really, new therapy - was easy. It became a platform for both therapy and education, all done through entertainment. Like everything, it is a balancing act. I think he would play on the iPad more if we let him. And while the iPad is a lot of things, it is not a replacement for real world experiences and interactions, nor is it a replacement for his sessions with his physical and occupational therapists.

My Motivation

My motivation for writing this is very simple: both of my children. Maya and Noah both challenge me in ways I could never have dreamed of. The iPad Book is dedicated to my hero, my son Noah. He works so hard, he makes me want to work harder.

Who Can Benefit From this Book

Getting started with any technology can be hard. At *BridgingApps.org*, we spend a lot of time trying to help people put it all together to make a positive impact on their children and loved ones. The iPad can be an amazing tool that can have a tremendous impact on a person's life, but putting it all together can often seem overwhelming.

This book was written with the following people in mind:

1. Anyone who is just getting started and would like a roadmap
2. Anyone who has already started and wants to get more out of the iPad
3. Anyone who needs a quick reference for the iPad and Special Needs considerations

Just like the *BridgingApps.org* website, I write for:

1. Parents of children with Special Needs
2. Therapists
3. Teachers/Educators
4. Caregivers

iPad Versus Other Devices

The iPad obviously is not the only portable, direct interface device available. Other devices, notably Android devices™, are on the market. This book does not address those devices or systems, which differ greatly from the iPad in design and available applications, as well as in other areas. That is not to imply that an Android device may not work for you should you choose to go that route. It's just not what this book is meant to address. Maybe the next one.

CHAPTER

What Is the iPad, What Can It Do and Why Should I Buy One?

You've seen the commercials, heard other parents and friends mentioned the iPad and think that it might be a good thing to try with your special needs user. Let's talk a little bit about the iPad itself - what is it, what can it do, and why should you buy one? - Before you take that next step and purchase an iPad. If you've already bought it, don't worry, we'll discuss set up in Chapter 4 and beyond.

What is the iPad?

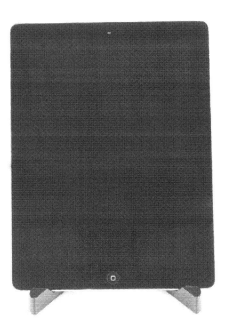

iPad 1 and iPad 2

The iPad is a tablet computer that runs on a mobile operating system. Because it grew from the mobile phone world, it has some very important design features.

1. Portability
2. Light weight
3. Easy to use on the go
4. Instant On
5. Wireless
6. Long Battery life

There is no doubt we as a society have become addicted to our phones. They are very powerful portable computers. Essentially, if you make one bigger, you have an iPad.   Why is that important for those with special needs? Simply put, it is one the first portable direct interface devices that is large enough to be used by those with special needs, but small enough to be conveniently portable and available at a relatively low cost.

Most other computer technology requires a person to manipulate a secondary device - a mouse or a keyboard - while looking at a screen. With the iPad, in contrast, you touch the screen and something happens. It is true that there are other touch screen devices, but none of them are as portable, and none of them have as powerful a computer for around $600.

The other major contributing factor to the explosion of the iPad in general, and with special needs in particular, is the availability of high quality content at very low cost. The mobile phone industry has created a strong demand for low cost, high quality content. If you told me a few years ago that less than $30 worth of apps could help my son begin to learn how to read, I would have told you that you were crazy. No one would have believed anyone would be creating such high quality software for that low a price.

What Can I Do With an iPad?

The iPad has been very useful for special needs children in many ways. The following are some of the more prominent examples:

1. Communication
2. Therapy
3. Education
4. Motivation
5. Self Esteem
6. Assistive Technology

Communication

The iPad has received a lot of attention in the world of Alternative Augmentative Communication (AAC). AAC is an area of assistive technology that deals with alternative methods of communication. AAC devices can be as low tech as flashcards or a picture board, and as high tech as a computer that can speak for you. There are two main systems within AAC: symbol-based communication and text-based communication.

AAC software can be broken down into two main categories: symbol-based and text-to-speech based communication tools.

Symbol-based communication apps use pictures to communicate words and concepts. Click on a picture and the associated word or phrase is spoken for you. The advantage of these apps is that if the user cannot read, the pictures are in fact a worth a thousand words. The primary disadvantage of pictures, though, is that they not universal across ages, cultures and cognitive levels.

Text-to-speech is just that - type a word or phrase into a text-to-speech app and it will speak the word or phase back to you and/or your audience. Generally speaking, text-to-speech apps can store a large quantity of phrases in a small space, allowing the user to have ready access to a wide variety of conversational elements. However, the user needs to be able to read and cognitively and physically manage (fine motor skill) the library of text.

Various pieces of software have been developed for the iPad that allow it to bridge the gap between very low tech and high tech (that is, high cost) methods of communication. Because the iPad is portable, has a long battery life, is relatively low in cost, and software development for it is easy, it is emerging as a great AAC platform. A single device can hold many different applications that may be used for communication in different circumstances. Because of the relative low cost, it can be obtained without going through the often difficult process of getting a medical device. This potentially makes the iPad an ideal platform for AAC.

Therapy

The iPad has emerged as a very versatile therapy device. The interactivity, the direct interface, and its fun and easy to use technology have all contributed to creating a multipurpose tool for therapists. At *BridgingApps.org*, we maintain a list of 100+ different skills that can be aided by applications, or "apps," on the iPad. They range from learning purposeful touch to recognizing complex patterns to using video to model behavior. The iPad's uses in the world of therapy are extremely wide-ranging.

I have seen occupational therapists use the iPad for fine motor development, such as finger isolation. I have seen cognitive development therapists use it for sequencing. Music therapists, psychologists - I have even seen physical therapists use it as a motivator for gross motor therapy.

That said, one of the most common therapeutical uses has been speech and language development. Not only has the iPad been an incredible medium for communication, it has had an even bigger impact in the field of developing communication and speech. At *BridgingApps.org*, all the apps we have reviewed are evaluated by a speech therapist. Speech/communication is central to the mission of assistive technology, and with so many high quality/low cost apps, the iPad's impact on the field of

Speech Therapy has been tremendous.

Life Skills Management

The iPad can be used to help manage life skills, from simple everyday aspects like email, contacts, tasks and calendars, to more specific special needs issues like visual scheduling, stress management, and event sequencing. The iPad can be used to manage money, to help understand what is appropriate attire for the weather outside, or to manage the routine of going to bed. It can help with dressing, potty training, and expressing emotion.

And all of this can be accomplished using various apps. Some apps are designed with therapy and skill-learning in mind, others are designed as productivity tools. You can think of the iPad as an endless Swiss Army Knife, if you need a tool for something, add an app.

Education

The iPad has also proven to be an effective technology platform and delivery method for a wide variety of educational areas. With the right programs, the iPad can provide a very interactive, immersive experience for a user. It is light and portable, so even the youngest of users can manage the device itself. Add all of this together with one more key ingredient - inexpensive high quality applications.

Why are applications, referred to as "apps," such a key ingredient? Think of it this way - an app is an experience, a lesson, an engagement mechanism. By having high-quality low-cost apps, you can take a simple device and create an almost endless variety of experiences for your user. The more high quality experiences the user can have, the more you can tailor those experiences to their precise needs. And the more tailored the experience is, the more value the user can get from it.

It is hard to imagine, but a $500 device with less than $50 of apps helped my son advance 12 months in cognitive development in just 4 months' time. If you said that was possible beforehand, I would not, and could not, have believed you. And I only do now because I have seen it with my own eyes. Of course, there were many additional factors in his success outside of the iPad, and I don't mean to imply that all children would experience the same dramatic improvement that I saw in my own child. But, that said, there is no doubt in my mind that the technology and apps were a catalyst.

Motivation

We can underestimate the value of cool toys as a way of motivating our children. For kids, toys are how they learn. With the right desire and delivery system, the toy can be a motivation in and of itself. I know parents who use the iPad as a motivator for their low-tone child to encourage him to walk on the treadmill. With my own child, we use the iPad as a reward for hard work in many of the therapies we have. His teacher actually puts the iPad at a distance away from him to encourage Noah to walk down the hallway at school.

Because the iPad is interactive, compared to more passive motivators like TV and video, I know parents who have used iPads to get their child to stay on the potty long enough to learn how to use the potty. The iPad captivated the child for a long enough period of time, and in a manner that videos and TV could not. Within a few short weeks, and after years of trying, they were able to potty train their child and no longer use an iPad for that purpose.

Self Esteem/Self Consciousness

When the iPad first became available, I was following the blog of a woman with Cerebral Palsy. Along with blogging and Tweeting several times per day, she acts as a consultant to make websites more accessible. And she does all this basically with one finger - that blows me away on so many levels. In her blog, she told the story about the night she got her iPad. She was attending a party, and when people approached her in her chair, and saw she had an iPad, they did not turn away. It was not a medical device that was helping her communicate; it was a device that was normal, every day technology - well, cool new tech at that point - but you get the point. I have heard this same story many times since, the concept that durable medical equipment turns people off, but common technology such as the iPad is more relatable, and less frightening, for typical people.

How does all of this fit into the equation and use of an iPad? Let me tell you another story. I know of a young teenager who uses an iPad and iPod touch to order food at McDonald's®. Eating there is one of her favorite things, and is therefore an excellent motivator. One of the reasons she enjoys going is because she can do it by herself, interacting directly with the outside world - no intervention, no special hardware or medical gear, just a cool iPad or iPod Touch®, some money, and herself.

Ubiquitous technology can be a vehicle to move forward to acceptance, coolness, and functionality in a way durable medical equipment simply does not. Commonplace technology allows for a relatable experience that allows you to focus on results, rather than further isolate the user. This provides a common experience - a connection - between the special needs and typical worlds, and this connection is what we all strive for, special needs or not. It can drive our self-worth, self-image, and ability to socialize and make friends.

Assistive Technology

"All technology, one way or another, is Assistive Technology, no matter what your need is, special or not" - Sami Rahman, right now.

Isn't the very definition of technology that it helps to make our lives easier? The iPad can organize your life, is a great way to communicate - it can talk, it can listen, it can take dictation - it is a warm book, a great spell checker, can take notes, take pictures, help with research, or act as a teacher, helper, or coach. There are any number of things it can do, and for that, it makes an ideal companion device. Whether you have a documented special need or not, the iPad is assistive technology available to a wide audience. It isn't a magic device, of course. Each user's experience differs, and a wide-range of factors will influence that experience.

The versatility of the iPad and its refined interface, built from the start with special needs in mind, allows it to be an ever-expanding and useful tool. As with all tools, though, it is just that. It has to be managed and used with purpose to yield the most effective results. But this tool can be altered and adapted in so many ways - from how you hold it, to changing the interface, to adding and using apps - which, throughout the lifespan of the device, can be combined in an infinite variety of ways to suit many different needs. Unlike most assistive technology that is either for a single use or is a specialty item, this technology can be used to address many different needs and build many different skills. That is unique to the iPad.

Why Should I Get an iPad?

If I told you that for a relatively small investment of $800 and some elbow grease, you could help someone speak, or with the same investment you could help someone develop at a cognitive rate of 200% or more, or with the same investment, you could help someone independently interact with the world around them when they could not easily do so before, wouldn't that be an easy investment? As you may have already guessed, the same $800 can do all three of these things.

The power of this experience for the parent and caregiver, though, is not the price or ease of use. The real power is that by going down this road with your special needs user, you are teaching yourself, you are learning how to incorporate therapy into all aspects of life. As a very good friend of mine pointed out, you don't normally experience education and therapy with your child. These are activities they do with other people. With the iPad, though, as you participate in these activities, you better understand the skills your child needs to develop and you are a bigger part of that experience.

Reasons Why to Get an iPad:

1. Improvement
2. More connected
3. Fun
4. Educational

   - Cognitive

   - Technology

The argument to focus on skills is simple. Skills fit into a therapy program, a professionally developed structure. As caregiver, whether primary or not, if you can understand the arc your user is on, you are more in tune and likely to be more effective. The fun part of the iPad can make the skill building seem more interesting. It can simply be more effective.

CHAPTER 3

What Do I Need to Buy?

Knowing which iPad to buy is important, however, you will soon realize that the accessories and other adaptive technology you may need to make the iPad more effective are just, if not more, important. In this chapter, we will cover the different types of iPads that are on the market, as well as the cases and assistive technology you may want to consider to make the iPad more effective for your user.

What Should I buy?

At the time of this writing, there are 6 models of iPads available: three are wi-fi only and three are 3G enabled. The only difference among the three in each category is the size of the onboard storage, or the amount of data it can hold at any given time. The sizes of onboard storage are 16 GB, 32 GB, and 64 GB. There are no other differences in the equipment on all 6 devices other than the 3G models are slightly thicker to accommodate the 3G antenna and chips.

The major questions you are going to need to answer:

1. Do I need a Wi-Fi or a 3G version?
2. How much storage do I need to buy?
3. What color?

Let's Start with the Wi-Fi vs 3G Question.

What does 3G do and do you want it? 3G stands for the 3rd generation of cell phone technology. That means that a 3G iPad has a built in cell phone technology that you can use to connect to the internet anywhere you can pick up a strong enough cell signal. This can have many advantages whenever you want to do anything that requires internet access, as you won't have to be near a wi-fi hot spot. For example, you can use the iPad as a portable GPS navigation device, as a video conference system, download apps, or use any app requiring internet access or with links to the internet for more information. With the 3G version, for example, you can use YouTube® anywhere you have 3G coverage.

Pros:

Access to internet anywhere, giving you the potential to make the iPad more functional if you need internet and are not near wi-fi access

Cons:

•   Cost

•   Monthly contract and data usage overage

•   Controlling content can be harder if you have internet everywhere

Considerations:

1. If you have an app that you must be able to use which requires internet access at all times, AND you don't have access to wi-fi everywhere you would use the app, then 3G is a good option
2. Everyone who has 3G loves it. But could they love the iPad without it? For most people, the answer is yes
3. High cost if you add in the contract
4. The next US version of the iPad will likely be 4G (that is, 4th generation wireless technology) and will have a higher resolution screen.

Alternatives to 3G

I was already using 4G on my cell phone when I purchased my first iPad and I thought it was both too expensive and unnecessary for my son. While I thought I could perhaps use it for myself, I did not want to sign up for a contract for my iPad, nor did I want to spend the extra money on the 3G iPad. Since I did not want the slower 3G connection, I bought the Wi-Fi version and got a contract for a 4G hot spot.

The advantages to the 4G hotspot:

1. Cheaper
2. Faster
3. It could work with any wi-fi devices (laptop, iPads, etc)

Disadvantages:

1. Another device
2. More to carry
3. More chargers

Another alternative is to use your cell phone as a hot spot, which you may be able to do with some carriers and plans. This can be a great alternative for a quick connection, but the disadvantage is that with most carriers, your phone can either operate as a hot spot or a phone, but not both at the same time.

Memory, or Onboard Storage

No one ever complains they have too much memory or storage. The iPad has three sizes of onboard storage:

1. 16 GB
2. 32 GB
3. 64 GB

This table can give you a sense of how much music and how many pictures you can store in the memory of each sized iPad:

IPad Version*	Number of Songs**	No. of Pictures***	No. of Movies****
16 GB (10 GB usable space)	2857 songs/ 168 albums	25,000	13
32 GB (28 GB usable space)	8000 songs / 470 albums	70,000	21
64 GB (60 GB usable space)	17,142 songs / 1008 albums	150,000	80

* I removed 4 GB per device assuming 2 GB for operating system and 2 GB for applications
** This calculation is based on 1 song = 3.5 MB of data, 17 songs per album
*** This calculation is based on average of 400KB per photo taken from iPad2 camera
**** 2 Hour movie = 750GB of space

Considerations for more storage:

1. If the device will be used for entertainment - for example, a teen with a lot of music, then you might want to consider getting a larger device
2. If you are a therapist or teacher, or will be working with a lot of children, then get more storage
3. If you travel a lot and want to carry more than 13 movies with you, get more storage

Reasons to not buy more storage:

1. Don't give an expensive device to a child who could break it. I feel a lot better giving my child a $500 iPad than an $700 iPad
2. You are going to be adding and removing content far more often than you think to keep your child interested in using the iPad and to keep up with their

development. Like toys, you will be removing some apps and content for a while, and bringing them back as needed.

Misconceptions about iPad storage:

1. More storage makes the devices work better. This is just not true. More storage usually just means you will have more things on your iPad.
2. Applications take up a lot of space. There are some apps - like a Sesame Street app that Noah loves - which contain a lot of videos that can take up space, but most apps are very small. You would have to have a whole lot of apps before you filled up a 16 GB iPad
3. Once you delete items from storage, they are gone forever. If you sync the iPad with iTunes®, you will always have a copy of the data on your computer. You can then use iTunes as a library to load and unload material.

Alternatives to Onboard Memory

There are a number of cloud storage solutions that can extend the amount of storage you can access on the iPad. A cloud storage solution just means that you have access to an online storage disk.

The advantages:

1. Can access from more than 1 device
2. Can extend the storage of any device that can access it

The disadvantages:

1. Only accessible if you have an internet connection
2. Not as fast as local storage
3. Cannot play video from remote storage, although I have seen some services that will allow you to play music.
4. Would not work very well in locations such as a car, where internet access fluctuates considerably

DropBox
Name: DropBox
Type of Service: Storage
Cost: Free for 2 Gb
Website: *www.dropbox.com*

Dropbox is a free service that allows you to bring all your photos, documents, and videos anywhere. This means that any file you save to your Dropbox will automatically save to all your computers, phones and even the Dropbox website. This is like having a 2 Gb thumb drive on the internet. If you need more space, you can upgrade.

Pros:

- 2 GB free, upgrade for more space

Cons:

- $120 per year for 50 GB total, $240 per year for 100 GB total,

- need internet access to be able to access the information

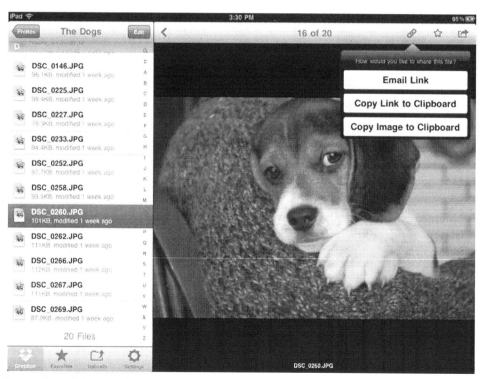

Screenshot of Dropbox App

Apple® iCloud®

Name: Apple iCloud
Type of Service: Storage
Cost: 5 GB Free
Website: *www.apple.com*

iCloud stores your music, photos, apps, calendars, documents, and more. And wirelessly pushes them to all your devices -- automatically. Think of iCloud as having iTunes on the internet. Buy a song or an app and have that app available on your devices all at once, after a little wireless syncing. It is a great idea, you don't have to keep backing up to iTunes. The catch is that you get 5 GB of space free, but the smallest iPad is 16 GB, so you will quickly outgrow the free space and you will have to upgrade to a larger plan. If you also have an iPod with 35 GB of music, you will not be able to fit into a 5 GB iCloud account. As of December 2011, the cost to add 10 GB is $20 per year, this would almost give you enough space to update 1 16 GB iPad (5 free GB plus 10 GB = 15 GB total). With extra videos and other content, you could have more data than 16 GB and use iTunes to swap it out. To do this wirelessly, you would need to upgrade to an even larger plan.

Pros:

- iTunes in the iCloud, larger storage than device can support

Cons:

- need internet access to be able to access the information, $20 per year for 10 GB more, $40 per year for 20 GB, $100 per year for 50GB

Notes:

- MUST be on iOS™5

Color

I think the color question is the easiest question to answer, as it is just a preference. There are only two choices: black or white. That said, white tends to show more wear than black. But since both devices are high gloss, they are both going to show signs of wear. In most situations, however, you will be buying a case to house the device, and there are a lot more colors to choose from in cases than in devices.

My Advice

My Advice: less is more in most situations. I have 3 iPads and they are all the black 16 GB Wi-Fi models. This allows me to control access to content outside and inside my home, and if anything happened to any one of the iPads, I would be out the least amount of money. I do spend a lot of time removing and replacing content, but that is not because I run out of storage; it is to keep up with the development and interest of my kids.

Physical Considerations

When selecting accessories, you will need to take the following physical considerations into account:

1. Protecting the iPad;
2. Accessories to help the user;
3. Assistive Technology and Adaptation

When deciding what to get, take positioning, mounting, cases, screen protectors, switches, stylus and other assistive technology into account to create a solution for your user. The following section will cover these items in greater detail.

Device Accessories

The first thing you are going to want to do is find a case that will both protect the iPad and be suitable for your user. This can be a balancing act, and you will have to decide what balance to strike. Keep in mind that what works when you start may not be what works long term, and that what doesn't work now may be what works later. As with most things in this world, experiment and find out what works best for your situation.

Protecting your iPad: Cases and Screen Protectors

There are a multitude of different cases and ways of protecting your iPad on the market. I am going to break down this topic into three main categories:

1. Protecting the iPad
2. Special needs concerns
3. Usability - Special Needs and otherwise

Protecting the iPad

The iPad itself is a relatively durable device. The aluminum body is both strong and protective. The glass screen is also fairly durable even without protection. Things you are going to try to protect the device from:

1. Dropping

2. Scratching/breaking the glass
3. Moisture, drool, liquids.

I would consider the following items in selecting a case:

1. How much protection do I need vs. how much protection do I want?
2. How are they going to use the iPad? Do they need a built-in stand, are they going to use it at a work table, in bed, in a wheelchair?
3. Bulk: If you are going to mount it to a wheelchair or table, then bulk may not be an issue. Bulk can be both a good thing and a bad thing. Think about how your child will be using it. If they are a teen on the go, are they going to have a hard time handling it? If it is too light, is it going to be too easy to throw across the room?
4. Weight: aside from size, weight may also be a concern. My kids, who are both very young, can't really lug around a big heavy iPad and case. In fact, some of the first cases we tried were so heavy that they dropped it even more. In other words, I needed to protect the iPad from the very case I was using to protect the iPad. That just does not make sense
5. Material. If you go with a leather case, as an example, is that going to hold up to environmental concerns like drool very well? Is cloth going to get dirty too often, is rubber going to be so tacky that it is to hard to rotate the iPad on the table from vertical to horizontal use?
6. Ports: All ports like volume and most importantly power, need to be accessible without having to remove the iPad from its case. Other than plastic bag type cases where the iPad is loose, you do not want to spend 5-10 minutes removing it from its case every time you want to charge the device.
7. **Cost:** Cases range from $3 for rubber sleeve to far higher for more sophisticated solutions.

There are two main ways to go when it comes to protecting the iPad: extreme cases that are sealed from the outside world and minimal protection. And then there's everything in between.
Extreme Cases:

Extreme Cases:

Let's start with the most extreme way to protect the iPad and that is to use a case that completely surrounds the iPad and seals it from the outside world. There are a number of cases on the market that can do this. Examples of a few of them follow.

Otter Box Defender Series

Type of Equipment: Case
Cost: $90
Website: *http://www.otterbox.com*

Description from the manufacturer's website: The OtterBox Defender Series for Apple iPad 2 is part of the our rugged line of cases, utilizing multi-layer technology and designed to withstand just about any environment. Don't worry about losing any access or functionality by wrapping your iPad 2 in the Defender Series; we've designed it so you can use all of the iPad's features right through the case. The inner polycarbonate shell has a foam interior to protect the back of your iPad from scratching, while the durable silicone skin works its magic by absorbing shock. The clip-on touch screen cover has a fold-out stand that offers up a convenient viewing and typing experience! **Please note: This case is NOT compatible with the optional iPad 2 dock.**

Pros:

- Less bulky than the Trident

Cons:

- Does not come with a screen protector

Trident Kraken for Apple iPad 2

Type of Equipment: Case
Cost: $50
Website: *http://www.tridentcase.com/*

Description from the manufacturer's website: Constructed from impact-resistant polycarbonate and double-enforced with a shock absorbing silicone inner-sleeve. Corners feature double-thick silicone for outstanding protection against drops and other impacts.Scratch-resistant clear PET screen protector shields the device from fingerprints, smudges, scratches and moisture while maintaining complete touchscreen interactivity.

Pros:

- Built in Screen protector, wings to hold onto

Cons:

- I have heard of users picking at the rubber

RJ Cooper Ultimate iPad Case

Type of Equipment: Case
Cost: $100
Website: *http://www.rjcooper.com/ipad-ultimate-case/index.html*

Description from the manufacturer's website: There are some of you that must have the ultimate in protection for your precious iPad. I do believe my Carry Case+regular Bumper Case provide as much protection as *most* of you need. But as I say, some of you want more.

Well, this is it. I've purchased and compared all the 'armored' cases I could find. The Incipio Destroyer was my winner. I adapt it so that it functions wonderfully as the ultimate iPad Carry Case, with shoulder strap, and Bumper Case for use with my iPad Mounts.

Pros:

- RJ Cooper just builds great stuff, he really knows what he is doing and it is very hard to go wrong.

- The shoulder strap is a very nice touch and really does make it the ultimate for carrying the iPad.

Cons:

- Cost

- May be more protection than you need

ZooGue iPad 2 Case

Cost: $50
Type of Equipment: Case
Website: *http://www.zoogue.com/*

Description from the manufacturer's website: The ZooGue iPad 2 Case Genius is the most functional case available for the thinner model of the iPad2. Made from Genuine Leather, the ZooGue Case is adjustable to any angle with its innovative velcro design. It provides access to all ports, cameras and speakers. The adjustable straps allow you to hang your iPad 2 just about anywhere. Securely mount it to your headrest in the car, or use it as a secure hand strap.

Pros:

- Very adjustable

- Has hand strap

- Can be mounted to a car head rest

Cons:

- Can be bulky for little hands

- Velcro attracts all sorts of cling-ons

Minimal Cases & Screen Protectors

I think a number of parents immediately gravitate to an extreme form of protection, and, in some cases, with very good reason. If you have a very aggressive child or one who drools a lot, or one who has a lot of fluids around, I would go for a case that is sealed and indestructible. I do have a child who has a lot of fluids and food around, and who does drool a lot, but because he was small, not very mobile, and not very aggressive, I went the other way and went minimal.

I am a big advocate of screen protectors. They can protect the iPad from scratching, drool, food, etc. There are three kinds:

1. Plastic Stick-on Self Application
2. Plastic Stick-on Professional application (same as above but require a professional to install, either with chemical or heat)
3. In Case screen protectors. (See Extreme Case section)

Plastic stick-on screen protectors you apply yourself are very common and can be bought at the Apple Store℠, online and elsewhere. They are made from various plastic materials ranging from the very cheap to helicopter wing material. In other words, from about $3 to as high as $20. For the professional application protectors, I have seen them for as high as $50 or so. I am sure there are all sorts of things that can be said about the grade of material, etc., but here is what I think you should consider:

1. **Glare:** You don't want something that is high gloss
2. **Clear:** You will want something that will not yellow. That said, depending on your loved one, it may not last very long
3. **Scratch resistant:** You want something that is designed to protect the iPad

I have heard from families who have gone down the professional route that they love the end results, they did not have to mess with anything, and the screen protectors are fairly bullet proof. If you not are not much of a do-it-yourself kind of person, I think this is a great way to go.

For me, I seem to always take the pain in my backside route, so I installed the screen protectors myself. I also don't find much difference in the quality of material, glare, cut, etc. between the cheaper $3-5 ones and the more expensive $20 versions, with this caveat: you do need to shop around. Cheap can just be cheap. I have bought some cheap screen protectors that just were bad, but I've purchased others for the same price that were great. Shop around. I have installed 20 plus so far and I use a $5 pack of 3 from Amazon®. My thinking is that if I screw up an install, or if my kids scratch the screen, I can replace them, they are cheap. This strategy may not work for everyone. And the fact remains that nothing will protect the device forever. If you choose to apply the screen protector yourself, that process is further discussed in Chapter 4.

Once you have the screen protected, then you have to worry about protecting the iPad during handling and, in the worst case, dropping. Our first case was a simple rubber case that was about $5 on Amazon. While this case did not have a stand of any kind, and was difficult to position, it did provide some protection and mostly gave Noah a way to grip the device so he could move it around and hold the iPad. He has fine motor issues, so we would typically position the device for him, but if he wanted to move it from landscape to portrait, he could hold onto it easily. It was the least bulky of the options. Further, it stayed put on the table where you placed it. (You will see the aluminum back of the iPad slides all over the place without a case.) This was a good solution for a while, but as he started to use the iPad for longer periods of time, it became clear that he needed a case with a built-in stand.

There are a number of cases with built-in stands. Most stands are fixed in only a few positions. I found this to be very limiting, so I set out to find a stand that could adjust to any angle and found the ZooGue. http://www.zoogue.com/products/iPad-2-Case-Genius-Black-Leather.html. There are two things that really attracted me to the ZooGue case. The first was that you could put at any angle because of the hook and loop design. This was great, as sometimes I wanted a steep angle, and other times, I needed a really shallow angle. The other reason why I liked it was the adjustable strap on the back. It could be strapped around my hand if I wanted to walk around with the iPad, or it could be loosened and strapped around the head rest of the car. All of the ports are very accessible, and the way it is designed, it almost has a bumper all the way around the iPad. On the downside, it is much bulkier than the rubber case; it is also heavy, and while this is not an issue with Noah, I have heard that if you put any kind of weight on the iPad while the stand is up, it can collapse very easily. This is a key point for kids who are rough or who don't know their own strength. There is no value if they think it is fun to keep flattening the case.

Other Unique Cases

There are cases for just about any need, budget or style. If you can't find what you are looking for right away, don't worry, it will come along soon. Here are a few examples of cases that might interest you. Keep in mind, you many need or want a number of different cases to handle different environments and conditions. For example, you may need a very rugged case for school and a lighter, more accessible case for home.

Keyboard Case

Keyboard cases are cases that have some type of built in keyboard. The primary advantage of integrating the keyboard into the case is that you get the best of both worlds. A keyboard when you want or need it and the screen when you don't.

Targus Versavu Keyboard and Case for the iPad 2

Type of Equipment: Case
Cost: $70-$100
Website: *http://www.targus.com/us/productdetail. aspx?regionId=7&sku=THZ084US*

Case and Bluetooth® Keyboard combined with rotating screen.

Pros:

- keyboard and case combined

- screen can rotate landscape or portrait without having to detach the keyboard.

Cons:

- Cost

iPad 2 Smart Cover

Type of Equipment: Case
Cost: $40 for cloth, $70 for leather
Website: http://www.apple.com/ipad/smart-cover/

Magnetic Cover that can be used to protect screen, come in cloth or leather.

Pros:

- lightweight

- will automactically put iPad into standby automatically

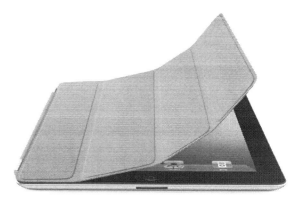

Cons:

- flimsy as a stand

- can often come off when you don't want it to

- does not allow for portrait viewing with kick stand

Other Accessories

There are a number of other accessories you should consider when you get an iPad:

1. Audio/Headphones
2. Physical Control over the home button
3. Stands
4. Keyboards

Headphones

You might want to consider getting headphones if your child likes to listen to videos or music and you just don't want to hear that song again. Headphones can be a great way for them to immerse themselves in the content. It can also help them block out extraneous noises and allow them to focus. Headphones are going to be a preference thing, and there are many to choose from. All headphones fall into two main categories:

1. Wired
2. Wireless

Some concerns you want to think through.

1. Volume control. It is possible the media is very loud and that headphones will boost the sound even more. My son likes everything on maximum volume. With boosted headphones, this potentially could damage his ears.
2. Content control. If they have headphones on, you will not be able to use your ears to monitor (no bad pun intended) what content they are viewing. For a child who has wireless access to the internet and is old enough or curious enough, this may be something you want to watch for.

Wired Headphones

A wired headphone has a cable connecting them to the iPad in order to power the speakers in the headphones. The advantages of wired headphones:

1. Can be more compact.
2. Do not need a separate power source
3. Can be less expensive

I like wired headphones. They are loud enough for most environments and seem to typically work without having to worry about charging, pairing and other technical issues. Consider me old school in that respect.

Wireless Headphones

Wireless headphones are cool. They are wireless, after all. But there are some downsides:

1. You always have to make sure they are powered
2. Battery life can be an issue
3. Pairing them and keeping them paired with your iPad can be a pain
4. They can be underpowered or too quiet, depending upon their design.
5. Can be very expensive

As I said, I like wired headphones, but they are not for everyone. Sometimes you need a headphone that has lot of power and can be adjusted separately. Since wireless headphones require their own power source, they often have all sorts of adjustments available. Just be sure that you match up the features of the headphones with the user and their specific needs.

Controlling Access to Applications

Sometimes is important to control access to application switching. There are times, especially with younger kids and those who are less developed mentally, that you will want the user to focus on one app at a time. There is not a software solution to this, so a company called Paperclip Robot created the Bubcap. It was originally designed to prevent toddlers from hitting the home button and changing apps all the time. The Bubcap is a small piece of plastic that fits over the home button. There are 3 different strengths of Bubcap plastic, and which you choose depends on your user's strength. The idea is that an adult would be able to press the home button through the cap, but someone with less strength or dexterity would not. This is a great product for anyone who uses an iPad in a group setting where they want to control the app, for example, therapists and teachers. It also great for toddlers. The issue is that you have to remove the Bubcap any time you want them to be able to free range and explore the rest of the apps on the iPad, and each Bubcap is a single use item.

Bubcap

Type of Equipment: Control Accessory
Cost: $4 per 4
Website: *http://www.bubcap.com*

Description from the manufacturer's website: BubCap home button covers are rigid enough to deter toddlers from pressing the home button, yet flexible enough that adults can activate the home button with a firm press. It's a similar concept to many child-proof caps for medicine bottles.

Pros:

- Prevents users from pressing the home screen button

- By controlling the home button you can control what the user can access.

Cons:

- Permanent. While it can be removed, once it is, it must be discarded, as it is not designed to be used sometimes and not others.

- This can prevent free range and exploratory use of the iPad

Tripod/Holder/Stand

Depending on a number of factors, such as the type of case you have, the support needs of your child, positioning, etc., having a separate stand can be of great value to you and your child. With Noah, because of his lack of mobility we have different "workstations" for him, one in the living room and one in the playroom.

There are essentially two types of stands:

1. Specialty stands for electronics; and
2. Do-it-yourself stands, like a cookbook stand.

There are a ton of special stands for electronics, some with built in chargers, some that are portable tripods. They range in price from $5 up. Things to keep in mind:

1. What do I need the stand to do?
2. Do I need it to be portable, i.e. back and forth to school?
3. Can I get a built in stand (to the case) to do what I need?
4. Will my child destroy a $100 super cool stand?

For the fourth reason in particular, some of the parents with whom I've spoken swear by cookbook stands they have bought at Michaels or Hobby Lobby for $5. The advantages are price and durability. You can have a number of them around the house or at school and not worry about them getting damaged, destroyed or misplaced.

Arkon Portable Fold-Up Stand

Type of Equipment: Stand
Cost: $14
Website: *http://www.arkon.com/iPad_accessories/ipad-stand.html*

Folding plastic tripod stand for iPad or other tablet

Pros:

- folds down

- can be set to a number of different angles

- light-weight

Cons:

- could get damaged if used by an aggressive child

Cookbook Stand

Type of Equipment: Stand
Cost: $6
Website: *http://www.amazon.com/
Fellowes-Study-Inches-Silver-10024/dp/
B00006B8HT/ref=sr_1_2?s=electronics
&ie=UTF8&qid=1314993686&sr=1-2*

Sturdy stand supports books, ipads and more at comfortable reading angle.

Adjustable; folds flat for storage. Contemporary wire design. Rubber end caps.

Pros:

- cost

- light-weight

- very portable

Cons:

- durability - could be thrown across the room

Wooden iPad Stand

Type of Equipment: Stand
Cost: $6
Website: *http://www.amazon.com/CaseCrown-Wooden-Reader-Redwood-Tablet/dp/ B003WM2LSC/ref=sr_1_1?s=electronics&ie=UTF8&qid=1314993618&sr=1-1*

Stand made of wood

Pros:

- made for iPad

- cost

- wood is a softer projectile

Cons:

- bulky

- not very adjustable

Tablet Stand Variable-angle Super-Stand

Type of Equipment: Stand
Cost: $50
Website: *http://www.rjcooper.com/tablet-stand/index.html*

Variable angle stand from RJ Cooper.

Pros:

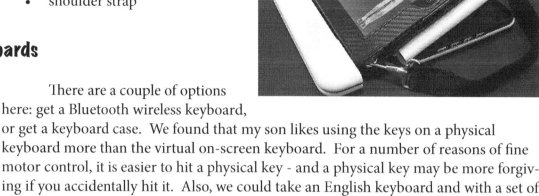

- built by RJ Cooper for special needs

- very adjustable

- shoulder strap

Keyboards

There are a couple of options here: get a Bluetooth wireless keyboard, or get a keyboard case. We found that my son likes using the keys on a physical keyboard more than the virtual on-screen keyboard. For a number of reasons of fine motor control, it is easier to hit a physical key - and a physical key may be more forgiving if you accidentally hit it. Also, we could take an English keyboard and with a set of very inexpensive stickers, make it into an Arabic keyboard. This way we can have an English keyboard and an Arabic keyboard, and we could keep them separate. In short, physical keyboards can be used with an iPad and should be considered for your user if appropriate for them.

Apple Wireless Keyboard

Type of Equipment: Keyboard
Cost: $70
Website: *www.apple.com*

Apple wireless keyboard used for both their computer line and mobile device line like the iPad.

Pros:

- small

- light weight

- designed to work with the iPad

- long battery life

Cons:

- cost, it is a little on the pricey side for a Bluetooth keyboard

Assistive Technology and Adaptation

Outside of the typical accessories, there are a number of assistive technology accessories that might help your child.

1. Switches
2. Stylus/Unicorns
3. Speakers
4. Attachment arms

Switches

If your child needs switch access for the iPad, there are a couple of things you need to know. First of all - and this is the most important thing - not all applications are switch-ready. In fact, most of them are NOT switch ready. The application itself needs to be designed for a switch and, to add insult to injury, not just any switch, but a specific switch. So apps have to be designed for YOUR SWTICH. Period.

Let me explain why. There is not a universal way for switches to communicate electronically with the device operating system and the applications themselves. This is mainly due to the fact that most switches work differently and there is no universal communication standard. For example, a physically connected switch communicates on/off differently than a Bluetooth switch. The most ideal situation would be for Apple (and Android) to build a standard into their mobile operating systems and from there it would be easy for software developers to add switch access. Since that is not the case at the moment for either mobile operating system, the app developer has to build access to a specific switch or switch interface and also has to design their software to use a switch.

Keep in mind that if you are using an iPad AND switches at the same time, you have two adaptation hurdles to overcome. I suggest working with your therapist resources when implementing a switch interface, iPad or not. Switches need to be the right switches, and they need to be positioned properly; otherwise, you run the risks of low adoption by the user and possibly even injury to them.

How Switches Work with an iPad

There are two primary ways to connect a switch to an iPad.

1. Bluetooth switch
2. Bluetooth Interface for a physical switch
3. Apps that are switches themselves

Bluetooth: What Is It?

Before we talk about switches, let's talk about what Bluetooth is. Bluetooth is a wireless method of connecting different hardware. A Bluetooth device has both a wireless transmitter and receiver built into it. Bluetooth is great because it is standard, so, theoretically, all devices that meet that standard can talk to each other. There are logical exceptions, for example, speakers do not talk to other speakers, microphones don't talk to other microphones. This makes it easy to connect different devices and you don't have to have custom software. It is also wireless, so you don't have any cables.

There are a couple of downsides to Bluetooth:

1. Range: you need to be within range of both devices, this is normally about 35 feet or less.
2. Power: you have to charge each device separately. One device cannot power another. This can be a big deal if, for example, the iPad, which lasts 10 hours, is matched with a speaker or switch that lasts only 2 hours.
3. Not all Bluetooth devices are of the same quality. I have had some Bluetooth devices match up and the sound quality or signal quality was poor; other times it was great. So just because it is a standard does not mean you will avoid any issues.

Bluetooth Switch

One solution to adding a switch to the iPad is to use a Bluetooth switch. A Bluetooth switch has an interface and switch built into one. This is nice because you only need two things to make it work: the iPad and the switch. The potential draw-back with a Bluetooth switch is that you can't use different switches. The two switches below have overcome this problem by also having 1/4 inch switch ports added so you can use any switch as well as the built in switches. This is a very useful feature.

Blue2™ Bluetooth Switch

Type of Equipment: Switch
Cost: $170
Website: *http://www.ablenetinc.com/Assistive-Technology/Switches/Blue2%E2%84%A2-Bluetooth%C2%AE-Switch*

Description from the manufacturer's website: Our new Blue2™ dual switch provides access to compatible iPhone, iPad, and iPod Touch applications via Bluetooth wireless technology. Simply sync the switch with your favorite Apple® device and activate the application's switch scanning mode to begin using the app hands-free. Blue2 supports both single and dual switch access through direct access using the two built-in switches, or plug in your favorite switches into the available ports to fit your individual needs.

 Note: The Blue2 is compatible with iPad, iPod Touch (3rd and 4th Generation), and iPhone (3GS and 4).

Pros:

- Two independent switches

- has two port for you to connect additional standard switches, I.e. ones you are already using

- Can also be used with a computer

 Note: This is a very versatile switch that can be used with many different devices mobile or computer.

Bluetooth Super-Switch

Type of Equipment: switch
Cost: $100
Website: *http://www.rjcooper.com/bluetooth-super-switch/index.html*

Description from the manufacturer's website: Switch access to iPads and tablets. For iPad, plug any switch(es) into it for cause/effect, switch timing practice, AAC auto-scan and step-scan, spelling, and any other apps on the ho-

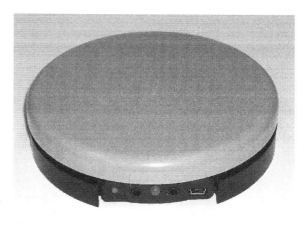

rizon! It works through Bluetooth 2.1 for simple pairing and range of over 50 ft. For iPad, any app that has been programmed for switch access allows access via switch(es). It has a lithium-ion battery that recharges through your USB port or USB AC charger.

Pros:

- has port to connect your favorite switch

Bluetooth Interface for a Physical Switch

If you already have the switches you like and they are set up the way you want them, then a Bluetooth interface is all you need to connect an iPad. The interface is just the addition of the Bluetooth transmitter and receiver for any brand of switch you already have. The key here is that the switch should be designed to work with the port of the Bluetooth Switch Interface, so you need to check that before you buy. The advantage for the user is that if they are already familiar with a switch set up, they can incorporate an iPad into an existing configuration easily. The adoption hurdle will be the application itself and the way it implements the switches. Experiment. Sometimes you just don't like some software.
Apps That Are Switches Themselves

Apps That Are Switches Themselves

There are a few apps that use the entire screen of the iPad as a switch. Predictable is a communication app that scrolls through each major element of the interface. Once a user gets to where they want, they tap on the screen, then it starts to scroll through parts of that sub-element. Take a keyboard, for example. For the rows of letters and numbers, Predictable scrolls through one row at a time, highlighting each row, numbers first, then the rows beginning with Q, A, and Z. Tap on a row, it then highlights sections of that row, 4 letters at a time. Tap on the highlighted section, then each letter in the 4 letter section. You can see that within 3 taps you can make a letter. In effect, Predictable turns the entire iPad into one big rectangular switch.

 Predictable
iTunes URL: *http://itunes.apple.com/us/app/predictable/id404445007?mt=8*

Predictable is a text-to-speech AAC application that uses word prediction to help simplify the communication process. Predictable can be configured to use the whole iPad as a switch or use a Bluetooth switch if desired and needed. By using a visual scanning strategy, the application can break down the interface to small enough units to make the user experience via whole screen touch very effective.

Screenshot of Predicatable App

Why Doesn't Someone Make Software to Turn Any App into a Switchable App?

This is a very good question and there are two main reasons:

1. Apple does not let software developers develop software that dramatically changes the interface of any of their devices. They believe, and rightfully so, that it could dramatically change the quality of the user experience.

2. The iPad does not technically multitask. Which means that it does not run two pieces of software at the same time. So you could not run the switch software and the application at the same time.

List of Switch Apps by Switch Interface

App	Interface	Type of Switch Access Available
TapSpeak Sequence	Bluetooth Cordless Switch Interface & Blue 2 Bluetooth Switch Interface	Single Switch or Direct Select; can be used at the same time
TapSpeak Button	Bluetooth Cordless Switch Interface & Blue 2 Bluetooth Switch Interface	Single Switch or Direct Select; can be used at the same time
TapSpeak Choice	Bluetooth Cordless Switch Interface & Blue 2 Bluetooth Switch Interface	Direct Select, 1 Switch Auto, 2 Switch Auto, 2 Switch Step, and Switch Swap Configuration for RJ Cooper's Dual Button Box.
GoTalk Now	Bluetooth Cordless Switch Interface	The GoTalk Now is the only AAC app to integrate accessibility scanning-either using another iPad or iPod touch as an accessibility switch (using Attainment Switch App) or your own physical switch with the RJ Cooper Switch Interface
Predictable	Bluetooth Cordless Switch Interface	Direct Touch, Auto Scan, User Scan, or Touch Anywhere

RadSounds	Bluetooth Cordless Switch Interface	Direct Select, Single Switch; can be used at the same time
Soundingboard	Bluetooth Cordless Switch Interface	Direct Select, Single Switch, Two Switch
Tap To Talk	Interface is built into this app	single-switch auto-scan; does not use external switch for scanning; you tap anywhere on the iPad to begin the auto-scan; then tap again to select, Single-Switch Autoscan

This list was created by a friend and special needs mom, Tina H., for BridgingApps.org

Stylus/Head/Mouth Pointer

A stylus is frequently used as an assistive technology for writing for any number of reasons. Not all traditional styluses work with the iPad because of the way the screen senses finger movement. The screen is triggered when your finger touches it. You would think this works by measuring pressure, so a pencil eraser ought to work. But it does not. The iPad screen works by sensing the very small amount of electrical current that flows through your body. Hence, a pencil with an eraser prevents the current from traveling through your body to the iPad.

Things to keep in mind when selecting a stylus:

1. Make sure the stylus is designed to be an iPad stylus. Typically, it has a metal body and the tips are designed to pass the electrical current from your hand to the iPad.
2. Make sure that any rubber grips can also pass a current. Adaptive rubber grips are often added to styluses to make them more usable, but you may need to experiment with a few to find one that will pass a current.
3. Make sure your stylus does not scratch your iPad or iPad protective screen. An all-metal stylus runs the risk of doing permanent damage to the screen, so be careful with your experimenting. Your iPad should have, at a minimum, a protective screen.

Not everyone has the use of their hands, and a head pointer can be the right assistive technology for those users. Keep in mind that you still need to pass a current from your body to the iPad. RJ Cooper has instructions for how to build a homemade head pointer or you may also buy one from his website. Notice there is a wire from the headband to the tip of the pointer. This is the key to allowing a current to pass from the body to the iPad.

Low Cost Stylus

Type of Equipment: Stylus
Cost: $3
Website: *http://www.amazon.com/Universal-Touch-Screen-Stylus-Silver/dp/B002BBJMO6/ref=sr_1_5?ie=UTF8&qid=1315237515&sr=8-5*

These are low cost generic stylus. They tend to very light weight and come in multiple packs.

Pros:

- Cost

Cons:

- I have heard mixed results from parents. Some like it, some don't.

- tip can be an issue

- small/thin bodies can be a grip issue

 Notes: Make sure when you are shopping that you buy a stylus designed to work with an touch sensative device. I would try to make sure it actually says design to work with the iPad.

Targus Stylus for Apple iPad

Type of Equipment: Stylus
Cost: $11
Website: *http://www.amazon.com/Targus-Stylus-iPhone-Tablet-AMM01US/dp/B003ZSH-KIY/ref=sr_1_1?s=wireless&ie=UTF8&qid=1315238821&sr=1-1*

We are currently using an adapted version of this stylus with Noah with good results.

Pros:

- heavier
- textured shaft
- pointer has gotten good reviews

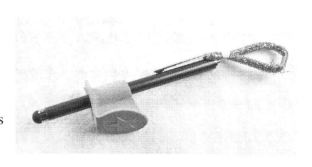

Cons:

- would still need to modify it for a larger grip
- may want a lighter stylus depending on user
- additional modifications

RJ Cooper Head Pointer

Type of Equipment: Stylus/Head Pointer
Cost: Free to Make
Website: *http://www.rjcooper.com/tablet-pointer/index.html*

RJ Cooper has instructions on his website to build a head pointer from common materials.

Pros:

- Low cost to build

Cons:

- need to have the comfort level to build your own assistive technology.
- fatigue may be an issue when using a head pointer for any length of time

iPad Mouthstick Stylus

Type of Equipment: Stylus
Cost: $40
Website: *http://www.etsy.com/listing/64832134/ipad-mouthstick-stylus*

Mouthstick is a stylus that can be used by placing it in the mouth. It is long, about 18" and is lightweight

Pros:

- lightweight

- well made

- effective even with a light touch

Cons:

- can be tiring, depending on user's muscle development.

 Notes: Positioning the device is important to reduce fatigue and prevent injury to the user

iPad Steady Stylus

Type of Equipment: Stylus
Cost: $40
Website: *http://www.etsy.com/list-ing/67270402/ipad-steady-stylus*

This is a T shaped hand stylus that can be used with the iPad. This is nice if your user is already accustomed to a T shaped pointer and can be used to help them make the transition more easily to the iPad.

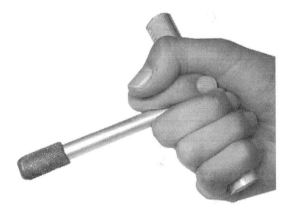

Pros:

- lightweight

- durable

iPad Stylus Sock Pro

Type of Equipment: Stylus
Cost: $11
Website: *http://www.etsy.com/list-ing/66258833/ipad-stylus-socks-pro*

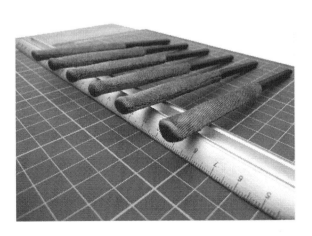

Easily make your own stylus or retrofit an existing stylus to work with the iPad

Pros:

- very inexpensive
- light weight
- durable

 Notes: Add the sock to the end of the stylus, there is a tether that runs up the length of the stylus and makes contact with the hand. What I like about this is you can use an existing stylus and adapt it to the iPad. The sock is a great conductor so you only need a lightest touch to make the stylus work.

Keyguards

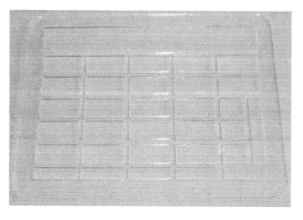

Keyguards are designed to help guide and control a user who may have a hard time controlling their index finger or pointer. Keyguards are plastic covers that can used on the surface of the screen of an iPad, touch screen monitor or Dynovox. There are cutouts in the cover where you can use your finger to activate an electronic button underneath. A keyguard prevents the user from unintentionally touching the screen. For some users, it is often the primary assistive technology that allows them to use a device at all. Because different software has different button layouts, keyguards are manufactured for particular pieces of software and have to be swapped out as the applications are changed on the device. For this reason, keyguards are designed for high usage applications, such as AAC and communications apps.

Lasered Pics Keyguards
Type of Equipment: Keyguard
Cost: $20 each
Website: *http://www.laseredpics.biz*

Lasered Pics produces many different keyguards for applications on the iPad. They will also create custom keyguards for their customers. They produce keyguards in a number of colors for low vision users. At the time of writing, they produce keyguards for the following applications:

1. Answers:YesNo HD
2. Assistive Chat
3. Grace
4. iClick iTalk
5. iMean
6. My First AAC
7. My Talk
8. Proloquo2go
9. Sono Flex
10. Speak It
11. Talk Board
12. Tap Speak Choice
13. Tap To Talk
14. Touch Chat

Pros:

- very inexpensive way of adapting the iPad into a full time communication device for a user who needs a keyguard

- keyguards can be attached to the iPad with a suction cup so they can be removed as needed

Cons:

- if you need a keyguard full time to use an iPad, you are basically dedicating that iPad as a single app device

- removing and reapplying the keyguard is likely not going to be very practical throughout the day

Above, image of red keyguard with Proloquo2Go layout. Note slot in between 2nd and 3rd columns to allow you to use your finger to scroll pages up and down.

Speaker

Adding a speaker may be necessary if you are using the iPad as an Assistive Augmentative Communication device. I have seen full-time AAC users with added speakers who swear by them, and others who feel they don't need them. Some considerations:

1. Volume need: You may not need a speaker in your house, but you may need one in a loud public area
2. Powered Speakers: A speaker that is powered by the iPad will not likely give you any more volume than the iPad's own speaker, so you will be looking for a powered speaker
3. Battery Length: The speaker should be able to last as long as the iPad or as long as the longest time you will need between charges
4. Cabled or Wireless: Do you want it to be wireless (Bluetooth) or will a wired speaker be better?
5. Mounting: How are you going to carry it around? Do you want to have it mounted to the case, to a wheelchair?

Mounting is a big consideration when talking to people about whether or not to add a speaker. There are specialty cases (for example, from RJ Cooper) that have the ability to mount a Bluetooth speaker or have speakers built in (for example, iAdapter Case). I have also seen a wheelchair with speakers mounted on it. With a wheelchair, of course, you are likely less concerned about bulk than if you were going to carry around an iPad with a shoulder strap or in your hand.

The other key issue is battery life: most consumer electronic speakers are made for personal use, for example, to listen to an iPod for a limited amount of time. So be looking for speakers that advertise a longer battery life. Ideally, you will want a speaker that lasts as long as, if not longer than, the iPad itself (or about 10 hours) before needing to be recharged.

iHome Speaker

Type of Equipment: Speaker
Cost: $70
Website: *http://www.ihomeaudio.com/iDM12BC/#features*

The iDM12 is an Bluetooth speaker system with a removable iPad stand and a built-in lithium-ion rechargeable battery.

Pros:

- both Bluetooth and wired connection,

Cons:

- 1.2 pounds
- USB charge only so you will need to get a USB wall jack for charging
- speaker battery life will vary depending on usage
- iHome does not publish any specs but my understanding is this is on the lower side of longevity
- less then length of a fully charged iPad

RJ Cooper Bluetooth Speaker (Motorola MOTOROKR EQ5)

Type of Equipment: Speaker
Cost: $100
Website: *http://www.rjcooper.com/ tablet-speaker/index.html*

Description from the manufacturer's website: The built-in speaker of the iPad is simply insufficient volume to allow the iPad and AAC software to function as an AAC device. Through the iPad's Bluetooth, which stays active even after sleep/wakeup, my iPad Speaker increases volume about 200%.

Pros:

- 3.5 oz, very light weight
- rechargeable battery lasts 2-3 days

- volume boost of 200%

 Note: Pictures shown where speaker is mounted to the stand and carrying case and iPad directly using velcro that is supplied with the speaker.

Attachment Arms

Mounting an iPad to a wheelchair or desk - in other words, positioning - can be a critical concern, especially if the device is being used for any length of time each day. Here are some questions to ask yourself:

1. Primary or secondary locations: Is the iPad going to mostly be mounted to a wheelchair or is the iPad going to be moved from wheelchair to workstation or play area at home? In most cases, you will want it to be removable from a work area, wheelchair, desk, etc.
2. How does the mount attach to the iPad? Is it easily removable, are the ports and buttons accessible, can I charge the iPad while in the mount, is the iPad protected enough?
3. How does the mount attach to the location? Will it damage the location, is it permanent, or does it matter?
4. Can I position the mount correctly to give the user the right support and position the iPad correctly?

Every user's needs are different, so here is where I would consult with a PT, OT, PM&R doctor or assistive technology specialist or other parents. In other words, get help, especially if you don't feel comfortable. If the positioning is done improperly, permanent heath risks can result. That said, you will likely need to experiment to find what works, what really works, and how to best set up the equipment.

There are attachment arms and mounts that are shorter in length for mounting on a table or desk. These may only have one elbow for positioning and long attachment arms, or may have mounts with a number of elbows to position the iPad at any angle. These can be used to attach an iPad to a wheelchair, a bed, a desk - you name it. I have seen a number of types of switch mounting equipment with accessories to attach an iPad.

How the iPad is mounted to the attachment arm and any protection it may or may not provide will be a concern. There is a balancing act between easy to use (i.e., easy to remove) and bulk (potentially protection). Some mounts are pressure clips that allow the iPad to be snapped in and out, but you will need to make sure that the screen is protected (screen protector) and that the iPad is positioned in such a way as to avoid drool, for example, if that is an issue. My point being, think through how it will be used as much as you can.

In the end, though, you will need to experiment until you find something that works for you.

Table Top Suction Mounts for iPad

Type of Equipment: Attachment Arm
Cost: $80
Website: *http://webstore.ablenetinc. com/table-top-suction-mounts-for- ipad/p/700400804/*

This product provides strong and stable mounting for your iPad 1 or 2 in either portrait or landscape orientation. The cradle securely holds the iPad steady while it's in use and still provides access to all controls and jacks.

Pros:

- simple solution

Cons:

- not flexible mounting system

Attachment Mount for Wheelchair

Tablet Mount System

Type of Equipment: Attachment Arm
Cost: $100 - $270
Website: *http://www.rjcooper.com/ tablet-mounts/index.html*

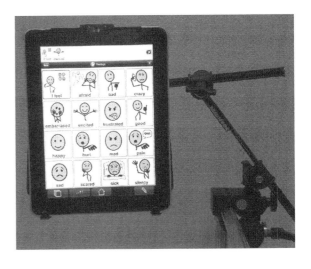

Table mount and attachment arm system.

Pros:

- flexible

- could have multiple arms with one mount

 Notes: This is a whole system and could be used to move the iPad from wheelchair to table to bed - 1 mount, a few different attachment arms, one at each major station.

Braille Interface

Braille interfaces connect to the iPad using a Bluetooth Connection. This interface prints the text from the iPad onto the interface screen in braille. The braille devices are more expensive than the iPad itself, but they can be used with other devices, such as computers and other Bluetooth devices. I do not have first-hand experience with braille interfaces, so I do not have any real insight on this topic. If you already have an interface, you might want to experiment. I suspect that implementation will vary from app to app, but this is just my gut talking.

ALVA EasyLink 12

Type of Equipment: Portable Bluetooth Display
Cost: $1600
Website: http://www.shoptelec.co.uk/docs/webshop.asp?act=item&itemcode=EASYLINK+12

The EasyLink 12 is a portable Bluetooth 12 cell braille display. It also has 6 braille input keys, 2 navigation keys and 1 joystick.

ALVA BC640
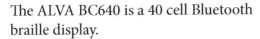

Type of Equipment: Bluetooth Braille
Display
Cost: $4200
Website: *http://www.visioncue.com/
braille-displays/ALVA-BC640-base-unit.
html*

The ALVA BC640 is a 40 cell Bluetooth
braille display.

ALVA BC680

Type of Equipment: Bluetooth Braille
Display
Cost: $9000
Website: *http://www.visioncue.com/
braille-displays/ALVA-BC680.html*

The ALVA BC680 is an 80 cell Bluetooth braille display that allows you to connect to
either two computers (Mac or PC) or a computer and a smartphone.

Checklists

What to buy Checklist:

1. What devices am I going to buy?
2. 3G? Yes / No
3. Storage? 16GB, 32 GB, 64 GB
4. Color? White or Black
5. What case?
6. Screen Protector?

Do I need?

7. Switch or switches? If you so what switch interface do I need?
8. Do I need a stylus or a head pointer? And which one?
9. Do I need an external speaker?
10. Do I need a Braille Interface?
11. Do I need a keyboard?
12. Do I need mounting arms, or desktop mount or tripod?
13. Do I need Headphones

CHAPTER

4

After You Buy

So you decided to buy an iPad. In this chapter we will cover

1. Un-boxing the iPad
2. Basic Setup
3. Understanding the various preference options
4. Managing access and setting up controls on the device, services, internet software, etc.
5. App basics
6. Apple's Accessibility Features

iPad Setup - First Time

Setting up the iPad is a fairly simple process. That said, depending on your comfort level with computers, plan on setting quite some time aside. Don't try to do this with screaming kids running around - you will want to be able to concentrate. I would also recommend doing this well in advance of any deadline you have for the iPad. You may need to get something you don't already have and that could take a day or two.

In short, to do's to setup an iPad:

1. Unbox the iPad - you will need an iPad
2. Install a Screen Protector - you will need a screen protector made for that iPad
3. Register the iPad with Apple - you will need internet access, a credit card or iTunes gift card and I would recommend a separate computer
4. Order Your First Application

To accomplish the above tasks, you need:

1. An iPad, charger, and sync cable
2. Screen Protector made for the model iPad you have
3. Internet Access
4. Credit Card or iTunes gift card to set up your Apple account
5. I would recommend a fairly new computer to sync your iPad with, that is, to backup your iPad
6. Quiet, Clean, well-lit work surface
7. Beverage of your choice

This process can take anywhere from 1-2 hours for an expert user or much longer if you don't have everything you need. You may also consider trying to do this over several sessions instead of all at once; this may allow you to absorb it better. Keep in mind that the moment your user really starts utilizing the iPad, it can quickly become a must-have tool, so spending a little more time getting comfortable up front with it is well worth the effort.

What Computer to Use With iTunes

 Tip: You will need a computer to register the iPad, back it up, manage applications, install new versions of the iPad software, etc. Since you will potentially be using iTunes a lot, I recommend that you pick a computer that:

1. Is well maintained, so you don't have to screw around with updates and other issues every time you want to do something with the iPad;
2. Has a fair amount of storage (for backups);
3. Is fairly new. You will have the iPad for years, you will use it a lot, so you will also use iTunes on the computer a lot. Moving this from one computer to another can be a mess. See Note about Syncing[Need to add section about syncing somewhere]);
4. Does not always have a kid on it.

Why, do you ask? Good question. The reason you want all of these things from your computer is that there is a relationship between the iPad and iTunes on the computer. Yes, you can get software directly on the iPad, but the system was designed to make iTunes on your computer the main library for the iPad. You can move stuff back and forth, you can use it to update the software, you can use it to backup the iPad. Considering that the iPad will become a very important tool for your child or your children, you need to make sure you have a long-term strategy to maintain it.

In contrast, let's say you decide to put iTunes on a older computer and it dies, you may lose everything like pictures, video, drawings even music that was created by your kids.

When to Add the Screen Protector

 Tip: The best time to add a screen protector to the iPad is when you first open the box; it is likely the cleanest your iPad will ever be. So make sure to have your screen protector ready, and a good, clean, well-lit work area ready before you unbox the iPad for the first time. Also, make sure you budget time to add the screen protector before you're ready to turn over the iPad.

As a side note, I have been known to curse a lot when adding the screen protector, you may want a beer or wine and a closed, sound proof room as well. iPad Introduction

Diagram of the iPad 2

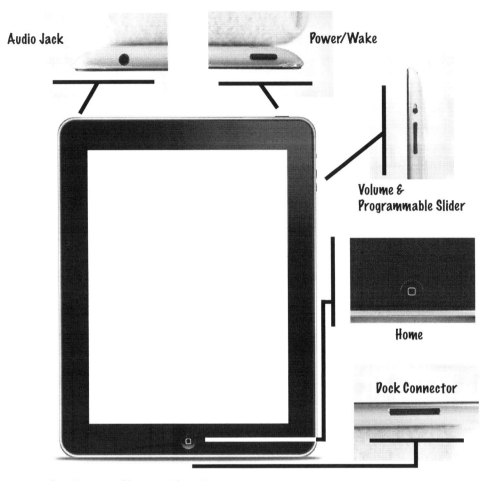

iPad Diagrams Showing Main Buttons

Front side of the iPad2:

1. **Light Sensor:** very small, above the camera; this is used to adjust the brightness of the iPad screen if auto-brightness is selected in the preferences;
2. **Camera:** the iPad 2 has two cameras; this is the front camera, with VGA resolution (640x480);
3. **Screen:** 9.7" screen with a resolution of 1024x768;
4. **Home Button:** the main navigation button on the iPad. With a single button push, it will allow you to exit a program, turn the device on from standby mode, and return to the main page when scrolling through pages of the main navigation area. With two button pushes in succession, it will launch the app

switch feature and allow access to some of the preferences. Three and four button pushes[Need to write about 3 and 4 btton pushes of the home button

Back of the iPad 2:

1. **Upper left-hand corner:** rear Camera, 1270x 720 pixels (720p);
2. **Lower left-hand corner:** speaker;
3. 3G built in antenna if you have a 3G iPad.

Top of the iPad 2:

1. **Upper left-hand corner:** 1/4" headphone jack;
2. **Upper right-hand corner:** power button.

Right Side of the iPad 2:

1. **Side switch:** default is speaker mute, but it can be programmed for rotation lock;
2. **Volume rocker:** top is volume up one level per tap, bottom is volume down one level per tap; press and hold volume down turns volume off instantly

Left Side of the iPad 2:

1. Nothing

Bottom of the iPad 2:

1. 30-pin dock connector port, provides power and sync. Can be used to attach accessories or video out cables.

Unboxing

The iPad retail box comes with:

1. The iPad itself
2. 1 10 Watt Charger
3. 1 UBS to 30-pin docking cable
4. Licensing information

After opening the box and examining each of the items, I would leave the plastic film protector on the iPad until you have a screen protector and are ready to install it.

Installing a Screen Protector

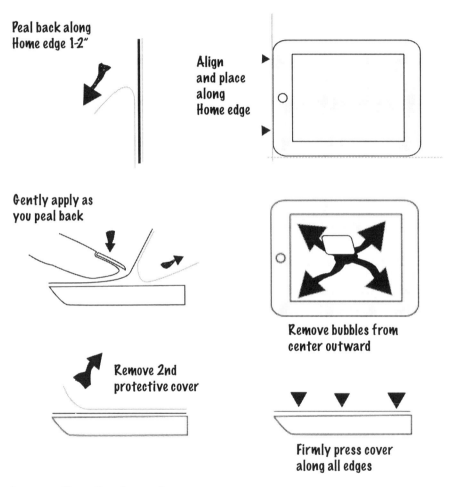

Peal back along
Home edge 1-2"

Align
and place
along
Home edge

Gently apply as
you peal back

Remove bubbles from
center outward

Remove 2nd
protective cover

Firmly press cover
along all edges

Diagram of Installing Screen Protector

A screen protector is the single best protective device you can install to protect your iPad investment. The good news is that a good screen protector is not very expensive and you can install it yourself.

What you will need before you begin:

1. A well-lit, clean work area
2. A screen protector and applicator (small plastic card that allows you to push air bubbles out from underneath the screen protector)
3. Clean, dry, lint-free cloth

 Tip: My recommendation is that you apply the screen protector immediately after removing the iPad from its protective plastic wrapper. Your iPad will never be that clean again.

Steps to apply screen protector:

1. Remove the iPad from its protective plastic wrapper;
2. Make sure there are no fingerprints on the front surface of the iPad;
3. Before removing the first of the two protective film sheets on the screen protector, make sure your screen protector fits the iPad by placing it over the iPad. Make sure the Home button is not covered and that the screen protector does not extend beyond the edges of the screen. With the Home Button hole lined up properly, take note as to where the bottom edge of the screen protector is. Is it lined up perfectly with the edge of the screen or is it slightly smaller? Remember this, as you will need this information in step 7;
4. Once you have checked fit and are ready to move to the next step, clean the iPad screen and make sure to remove any lint or dust that could get trapped between the iPad screen and screen protector;
5. Face the iPad with the Home Button on your left side and the camera on your right side (if you're right-handed; reverse if you're left-handed) with the iPad in landscape orientation. You may want to place it on a towel so it does not move around;
6. Remove the first inch of the first of the two film layers on the side of the screen protector with the hole cut out for the Home button, peeling it away from the adhesive side. Once removed, it should expose the adhesive side of the screen protector which should be clearly marked as the one to stick to the iPad screen. If in doubt, read the instructions that came with your screen protector;
7. In the corner closest to you on the left hand side, gently put down the corner of the screen protector. Using your finger, lightly hold down this corner while aligning the bottom edge of the screen protector to the bottom edge of the iPad. It should be the same distance from the bottom as in your practice run in Step 3. If all is not well, you will know it and will likely be cursing, so carefully remove the screen protector and start over. You should be able to salvage

the unused screen protector if this is done carefully. If all is well, you should have your finger in one corner and the home button properly aligned on the iPad. Run your finger down the edge of the iPad where the screen protector and iPad meet from corner to corner to remove any air bubbles;

8. With your right hand, slowly remove the remaining film on the screen protector by pulling gently on the protective film, while simultaneously using your left hand to gently apply pressure to the freshly exposed screen protector. The left hand should be in continuous motion from left to right to prevent any air bubbles from developing. I have found that my left hand is best about 1.5" from where the film and screen protector meet. My right hand moves away farther as the film gets longer. You will likely have to stop mid-way or more to readjust your right hand to grip the film closer to the parting point. The key is to make sure you are working the air out from underneath;

9. Once the screen protector has been placed, used the applicator card to remove any lingering air bubbles from the center outward;

10. As a secondary application step, I would use your thumb and go over the entire screen protector using firm pressure. This second pass helps to make sure the adhesive has properly made contact with the iPad screen;

11. Once you have applied the screen protector, remove the second protective film on the outside. I have found that sometimes this will pull up the screen protector, so when doing this last step I am careful and make sure I go slowly, using my finger to apply pressure to the screen protector in the corner where I am pulling.

If all else fails, you can start again with a new screen protector. If you find this is really not for you, here are a few alternatives:

1. Find a kiosk in the mall that specializes in screen protectors and have them do it;

2. Use a screen protector with a different type of application method.

Skinomi TechSkin

Type of Equipment: Screen protector
Cost: $20
Website: *http://www.skinomi.com/apip2p.html*

Unlike a dry adhesive screen protector, Skinomi screen protectors are applied wet and then allowed to dry overnight. This may seem counter-intuitive, but it is how window tinting is done on cars.

Pros:

- very easy to apply

- remove bubbles

- repositionable

- very long lasting and durable

- closest to no screen protector I have seen on the market

Cons:

- cost

- it takes 24 hours to dry

Registering iPad with Apple

Before you begin:

Make sure you have selected a good computer for set-up, see Note on Before You Begin at the beginning of this chapter. You will need:

1. Computer with iTunes
2. Internet Connection
3. An existing Apple ID, or you will need to create one

   - You will need a valid credit card to create an Apple ID

   - If you are registering an iPad on behalf of someone else and are creating and maintaining an account for them, you may want to use a pre-paid credit card instead of your own.

To register your iPad:

Here is how to registering your iPad with Apple:

1. Turn on the iPad using the power button on the top right hand side.

2. Plug the 30-pin dock connector cable into your iPad, then plug the USB connector on the other end into your computer.

3. Launch iTunes if it did not already do so.

4. Once the iPad is recognized it will ask you if you want to register. Select continue.

5. Next you will read over and agree to Apple's iPad Software License Agreement, then select continue.

6. Enter your Apple ID or create one

7. Enter Registration Details: From your Apple ID, it will use the information on file; make corrections as needed.

8. Find My iPad: Set up **Find My iPad**. See below section on **Find My iPad** for more information on what this service is, but you should set it up; it is a free service.

9. Set up a new iPad or do it from a backup: Since this is the first time you are setting up this iPad you will select **Set up a new iPad**

10. Naming and Basic Settings:

   • Name your iPad: Give your iPad a meaningful name. I used "Noah's iPad"

   • You will need to decide if you want to

   • Automatically sync music and videos

   • Automatically add photos

   • Automatically sync applications

   • My recommendation is to only select **Automatically sync Applications to the iPad** until you have developed a plan around video, music and photos.

11. Sync Content: Here you are able to pick exactly what you want copied over to the iPad and check for new updates. You can choose to sync:

   • Apps

   • Music

   • Videos

   • TV Shows

   • Podcasts

- iTunes U®

- Books

- Photos

- Each tab gives you complete control over what you have and want on your iPad; my advice is at this early stage is that less is more.

12. Apply Settings: Once you select the **Apply** button, your settings will be saved and your iPad will back itself up to your computer. Any content you select in iTunes will be copied over to your iPad. Depending on the volume of content, this can take several minutes.

13. Once complete, eject your iPad using the **Eject Button** in iTunes, detach all cables and hit the power button on the iPad. Once it boots up, you are ready to use it.

Find My iPad

Find My iPad is a free service through Apple's MobileMe® network for users of Apple devices (iPad, iPhone® and iPod Touch) running iOS 4.2.1 or later. MobileMe is a paid service, but users who register from their iOS 4.2.1 or later devices can do so for free. The service allows you to

1. locate your device on a map
2. lock it remotely and set a 4 digit passcode
3. display a message
4. play a sound
5. remote wipe the device of all of its data.

Since it is free and you cannot set it up after the fact, it is something you should consider doing during your set-up process. If your iPad is lost or stolen, it could assist you in finding the device, or at least allow you to prevent someone from obtaining too much personal information about you and your loved ones.

Setting Up Wi-Fi on the iPad

Unless you've purchased the 3G model, the only way to get internet access on the iPad is via a wi-fi internet connection. You will want internet access on your iPad in order to get applications directly on the iPad and to use any applications that require internet access, such as email, calendar, or an internet browser.

What you will need before you begin:

1. An iPad
2. A wi-fi internet network
3. The passcode to your wi-fi internet network

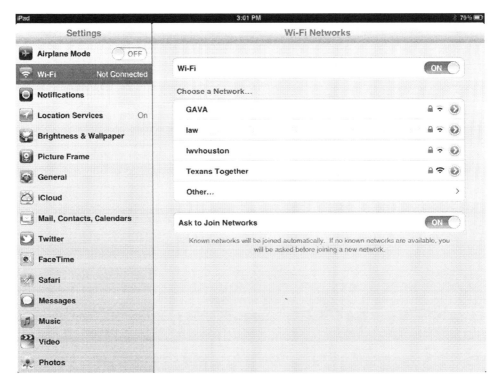

Screenshots of Wi-Fi Settings

Setting up for wi-fi internet on your iPad:

1. Launch the Settings application on the iPad
2. Select **Wi-Fi Settings**
3. Turn on **Wi-Fi**
4. From the list of available wi-fi networks under **Choose a Network**, select your wi-fi network
5. Enter your wi-fi network passcode, if required
6. Once you are connected to a network, your tool bar at the top will have the familiar Wi-Fi icon in the upper left hand corner next to the words IPAD.

Setting Up 3G on the iPad

Verizon and AT&T

In the United States, there are two carriers for the iPad, Verizon and AT&T. Verizon uses CDMA technology; AT&T uses GSM. GSM is the most popular standard and is available elsewhere around the world, so if you are an international traveler and are willing pay the roaming rates when you travel, consider AT&T. Technically, CDMA is newer technology and is theoretically better at handling the tower-to-tower signal transfers. In practice, though, for data I have not found that CDMA is any better at handling tower-to-tower transfers. This would only really affect you in car rides anyway, so I am not sure if either is a clear winner. It will essentially come down to coverage in the areas you like to frequent the most and how many towers each carrier has in your travel area.

US Data plans As of September 2011

Verizon:
2 GB = $30 per month, 5 GB = $50 per month, 10 GB = $80 per month

AT&T:

200 MB = $15 per month, 2 GB = $25 per month, 4 GB = $45 per month

UK Plans as of March 2011

Vodafone 2 GB = £27 per month
T-Moblie 1 GB = £25 per month

Japanese Plan as of March 2010

Softbank Unlimited = 4,410 yen per month

Egyptian Plans as of February 2012

Vodafone 150 MG = 25 LE
Vodafone Unlimited = 250 LE

App Basics

One of the first things you are going to want to do is to add some apps to your iPad. An **"app,"** short for application, is a program that will allow you do more than the basic programs that came with the iPad. There are three varieties of apps in terms of cost. Some apps are free for full versions, some have free "lite" versions and paid full versions, while others are paid full versions. Since this book is all about special needs users and the iPad, it is safe to assume that you will want to download and install apps for your user. Great, we will get to that, but let's start with some basics.

You already know that an app is an application. So where do you get these apps? You can get them all from one place: the Apple App Store. There are two ways to get them from the Apple App Store to your iPad. The first way is to purchase them through iTunes on your computer then sync them to iPad, or you can buy them directly on your iPad using the App Store application on it. In both cases, though, you will need a connection to the internet.

Apple ID and Buying Apps

The key to the whole app buying thing is the Apple ID you use. When you buy an app or download a free app, the Apple ID records your purchase, in the case of apps that cost money, or order, in the case of free apps, of that particular app. Basically, Apple ID YYYYY bought app ID ZZZZZ. You then download and install this app. When you sync with your iTunes account on the computer, it says, "oh, you bought app ID ZZZZZ," and records that in iTunes. It backs up a copy of the installed app for later use. At any rate, in our house I have three iPads, and since they are all used by the kids - I only occasionally get to actually use mine - I use one Apple ID and set-up my children's two iPads to be identical. My thinking is that this should make my life easier, reduce fights, etc. While my kids' ages and interests are different, they often take each other's iPads, so I just made them the same.

Another thing about buying apps that you should know is that once you buy an app, you are also buying all future versions of the app. This includes free apps as well. This is a great thing. As the apps develop, you get all new versions, if they find a bug and fix it, you get the fix, and if they add a new feature, you get that too. This also means that you will be regularly updating apps and will want to have a routine for updating and backing up your iPad.

One Apple ID or More?

If you only have one iPad then don't worry about separate Apple IDs, but if you already have multiple Apple IDs, or if you want to manage pools of content separately, or, for example, want have someone other than you (like a teenager) be able to buy their own content, then you will likely want to have different Apple IDs. The reason I bring this up now is that you will want to plan what accounts you use to buy your apps. Separate accounts will not allow you to share apps, but they will allow you to manage different universes of content separately. A single account will allow you to share apps between devices, but you might not want another person to have full access to your account. You will want to consider these trade-offs now before you start.

How to Buy an App from iTunes

To buy an app using the iTunes application:

1. Launch iTunes on your computer
2. Login to the iTunes Store® using the proper Apple ID account
3. In the upper right hand corner you will see a search bar. Type in keyword words to describe the app you are seeking. In my example, I used the word "spelling." In iTunes, the results are more than just iPad apps, they can be pod casts, iPod®/iPhone apps, they can be video, or music, university lectures or books. This can be both good and bad, it all depends upon what type of result you want.

Screenshot of iTunes Login Dialog

Understanding iTunes Search Results

Screenshot of iTunes Search results

In the example above, I searched for the word "spelling." When you use the search bar in the upper right hand corner of iTunes, you are searching the entire iTunes store and all of its content. This includes:

1. Music
2. Movies
3. TV Shows
4. Applications for both the iPod/iPhone and iPad
5. Books
6. iTunes U (iTunes University)

In the main results box, you are given the results organized by content type. Under the **Filter By Media Type** header, you can choose to further filter your results by a particular type. You can only select or filter one category at a time. Since we are talking about apps, when you click on the Apps filter you will find that the results are divided by iPhone Apps (also in this category are iPod Apps) and iPad Apps. The distinction between these is really determined by screen size. Think of it as small (iPhone/iPod) and large (iPad) apps.

Next to the main section heading is the **See All** link, click on that and you will see all results under that section. The results are presented in a multi-page format, so you may have to scroll through multiple pages to review all of the results of your search. Select an app title to see a full page of information about the app.

Understanding the App Page in iTunes

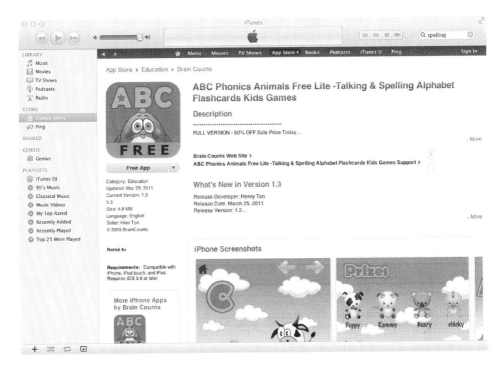

Screenshot of App Results in iTunes

This is a results page once I clicked on an App after searching for "spelling" in the iTunes store.

At the very top of the results window, we have **App Store > Eduction > Brain Counts.** This uppermost bit of information gives you a little hint as to how Apple organizes its information. The first element, **App Store**, means that the result is in the application store. The second element, **Education**, means that it is in the category of Education, the third element means that this app is organized around its developer, Brain Counts. That information is confirmed later, as I will show you shortly.

The specific information for the app is broken down into two columns. In the Left Column we has the following information about the app:

1. **App Icon**, in this case, the blue bird
2. The **cost** of app, in this case, free
3. **Category** in which the app belongs, in this case, Education
4. The last time it was **updated**: Mar 29, 2011
5. Current **Version** of the app: 1.3 (stated twice, not sure why)
6. **Size** of the app: 4.8 MB (megabytes)
7. **Main Language** of the App: English
8. **Seller's Name:** Hien Ton
9. **Copyright information:** 2009 BrainCounts
10. **Age Rating:** 4+
11. **Compatibility** with which devices and which operating system versions
12. **Other Apps** by this developer or another similar apps (in other words, buy more stuff)

In the Right hand column of the app-specific page, you have the following information:

1. **Application Title:** ABC Phonics Animal Free Lite - .....
2. **Description:** This is a long section with lots of keywords, descriptions and lots and lots of marketing language
3. **What's New in Current Version:** This section is should list what is new in the most current version, but it often contains more marketing stuff
4. **Screenshots:** You can usually get a good idea of how the program looks by reviewing the screenshot. Your eye will become keener once you get more familiar with apps in general.
5. **Customer Reviews:** There is both a star rating system and customer comments. Reviews are kept for all versions of the app even if there has been an update. Personally, I don't put too much stock in the reviews. It is not that the reviews are bad - they are a great idea - it is that when I read a review from the parent of a typical child, it often does not apply to my son's needs or how we want to use the app. Keep this in mind when you read the reviews. So if you read a review, either good or bad, think about whether or not that particular aspect is important to you and your user. I use the review as a general guideline to the quality of the app. I look for major flaws, lots of bugs, or other impediments to using the apps.

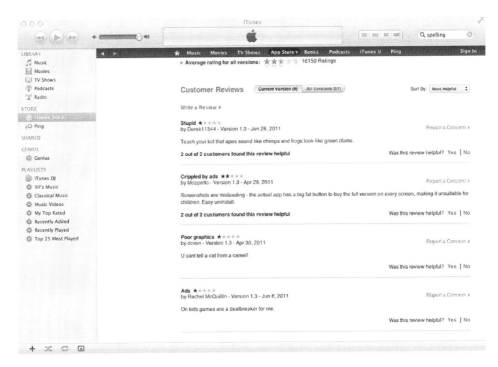

Screenshot of iTunes Apps Results Comments

Buying and Downloading Apps from iTunes

Buying apps from the iTunes store is easy. Below the icon on the app in the upper left hand corner is a price bar. If the app is free, it will say free; if the app is for a fee, it will tell you the price. In the world of Apple apps (both in the App Store on the iPad and in iTunes), you "purchase" apps. Even if the app is free, the process is still the same. The steps are as follows:

1. Click on the **Price Bar** below the app icon
2. iTunes will make sure you are logged in with your Apple ID; if you are not, log in.
3. If the app costs money, you will be asked to confirm your purchase. If the app is free, you will skip to the next step.
4. Once your purchase has been authorized, you will begin the download process. Very similar to downloading music or movies, you will see the name of the app appear in the uppermost status bar (top area in the center of iTunes) with a status bar showing you the download in progress.
5. You have now bought the app.

Note: Here is the thing, just because you bought the app and downloaded it to the computer, it does not mean that it is on the iPad. You now need to sync the computer and the iPad to transfer the information.

Pros and Cons of Buying Apps in iTunes

There are pros and cons of buying apps in iTunes.

Pros:

• Using a computer, a large monitor and a keyboard can make it much easier to do a search

• You will see other content, such as TV Shows and Books, that may be interesting to you

• Your apps are backed up even before they get to the iPad

• You don't need the iPad to search for apps

Cons:

• It is a two step process, you need to download to your computer, and then download again to the iPad

How to Buy an App Using the App Store on the iPad

You can buy apps directly on the iPad if you have an Apple ID and the iPad has access to the internet. Launch the App Store application on your iPad. You will get a screen that looks something like the screenshot on the next page.

I will be covering the App Store application on the iPad in more detail than iTunes because you will likely be using this app quite a bit and it is an application dedicated to finding apps for the iPhone and iPad, whereas iTunes is broader in its search. The good news is that the two applications are very similar, and the information is transferable.

Screenshot of App Store Home Screen

The main page of the App Store application can be broken down into four sections:

1. **Header:** along the top you will find three buttons and a search bar:

   - **New** - tap here and get a list of new apps

   - **What's Hot** - tap here and get a list of popular apps

   - **Release Date** - tap here and get a list of all apps released that day.

2. **Feature Area:** here you will find a few apps that Apple really wants you look at
3. **New and Noteworthy**: here will find more apps Apple really wants to you look at
4. **App Store Menu:** along the bottom you will find a menu of the major areas of the App Store:

   - **Featured** - where you are now

   - **Genius** - tap here and you get application suggestions based upon previous purchases

- **Top Charts** - tap here and you will get three lists: **Top Paid Apps**, **Top Free Apps**, **Top Grossing Apps**

- **Categories** - list of apps based on the various app categories, for example, Education and Games

- **Purchased** - tap here and get a list of all apps you have purchased, whether paid or free

- **Updates** - tap here to update any app that has a new version.

Understanding App Store Search Results

Screenshot of App Results in App Store

When you run a search in the App Store, unlike searching in iTunes, the results are only for iPad and iPhone apps. You do not get results for music, movies or other content. Depending upon what you are searching for, this can be a good or a bad thing. To further refine your search, you can use the filters at the top of the search bar. You can also change sort order by using the "Sort By" drop down menu. Combining the sort order and filters can further narrow your results. To see a full list of apps in either the iPad category or the iPhone category, tap on the "See All" link next to the corresponding category title. To see an app, tap on the app icon to launch the full app description screen. To install an app directly from the results screen, tap on the price, the price will turn green and change to install. Tap again to start the authorization, download and installation process.

Understanding the App Page in the App Store

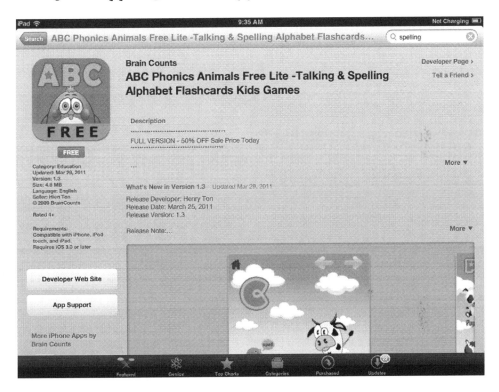

Screenshot of App Results in App Store

Here is a results page once I clicked on an App after searching in the App Store. The rest of the page is broken down into two columns. This is very similar, if not almost identical, to how the information appears in iTunes. In the Left Column we have the following information about the app:

1. **App Icon**, in this case, the blue bird
2. The **cost** of app, in this case, free
3. **Category** the app belongs to, in this case, Education
4. The last time it was **updated:** Mar 29, 2011

5. **Current Version** of the app: 1.3
6. **Size** of the app: 4.8 MB (megabytes)
7. **Main Language** of the App: English
8. **Seller's Name:** Hien Ton
9. **Copyright information:** 2009 BrainCounts
10. **Age Rating:** 4+
11. **Compatibility** with which devices and which operating system versions
12. **Other Apps** by this developer or another similar apps (in other words, buy more stuff)

In the Right hand column is the following information:

1. **Application Title:** ABC Phonics Animal Free Lite - .....
2. **Description:** This is a long section with lots of keywords, descriptions and lots and lots of marketing language
3. **What's New in Current Version:** This section is should list what is new in the most current version, but it often contains more marketing stuff
4. **Screenshots:** You can usually get a good idea of how the program looks by reviewing the screenshot. Your eye will become keener once you get more familiar with apps in general.
5. **Customer Reviews:** There is both a star rating system and customer comments. Reviews are kept for all previous versions of the app as well. Personally, I don't put too much stock in the reviews. It is not that the reviews are bad - they are a great idea - it is that when I read a review done by the parent of a typical child it often does not apply to my son's needs or how we want to use the app. Keep this in mind when you read the reviews. If you read a review, either good or bad, think about whether or not that particular aspect is important to you or your user. I use the reviews as a general guideline to the quality of the app. I look for major flaws, lots of bugs, and other impediments to using the apps.

Buying apps from the App store is easy. It is almost identical to buying an app in iTunes, except you are buying the app using the iPad. Below the icon on the app in the upper left hand corner is a price bar. If the app is free it will say "free;" if the app is for a fee, it will tell you the price. In the world of Apple apps (both in the App Store on the iPad and in iTunes), you "purchase" apps. Even if the app is free, the process is still the same. The steps are as follows:

1. Tap on the **Price Bar** below the app icon. If you are in list view you can tap on the Price Bar beside the app icon.

2. If the app costs money, you will be asked to confirm your purchase by entering your Apple ID password. If the app is free, you will skip to the next step.
3. Once your purchase has been authorized, you will begin the download process. On the Home Screen you will see the app icon appear. It will be transparent and have a status bar across the lower third of the icon showing you the progress of the download. When the download is complete, the icon with be solid.
4. Tap on the app icon to launch the app.

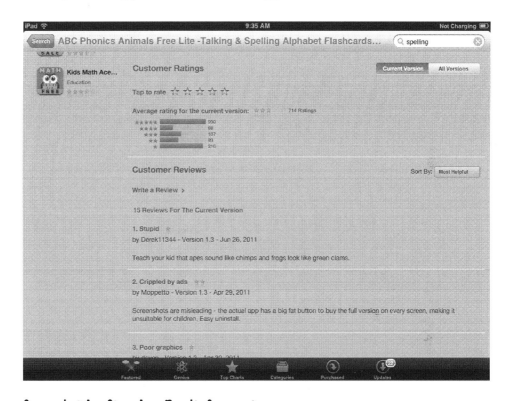

Screenshot App Store Apps Results Comments

Pros and Cons of Buying Apps in the App Store

Pros:

• One step process, once you buy the app, it is installed during the process

• You don't need a separate computer

Cons:

- The iPad has a smaller screen to review search results

- You cannot are see other content such as TV Shows and Books that may be interesting to you

- Your apps not are automatically backed up.

Tour of the App Store

Screenshot of Menu Bar of App Store

While you will likely mostly be searching for apps via keyword, the App Store does have a number of other ways to find apps. Along the bottom on the App Store application are the following menu items:

1. **Featured App**
2. **Genius**
3. **Top Charts**
4. **Categories**
5. **Purchased**
6. **Updates**

Featured App

When you first open the App Store, you will be presented with the Featured application page. Here is where Apple puts the "Hot" apps. While I am not sure they fully disclose what criteria they use to determine which apps are "hot," I am sure there is a ton of computer and marketing power behind what you see. There are three main areas of the page.

Along the top tool bar are three buttons. When selected, they will show you the categories called **New Apps**, **What's Hot**, and **Release Date.** Under the **New** button you get a list of new apps, or what the marketers want you to see. **What's Hot** is a list of apps that are selling well or getting downloaded a lot, in the case of free apps. **Release Date** are all apps released on the current day. There can be a ton. While you are going to find a lot of interesting apps in all three of these lists, it will not likely be the first place to look for apps for special needs users.

In the middle is the main feature area. This space is here to highlight a handful of apps. While it is interesting to look at as you pass by, it is not likely where you are going to find a lot of apps relevant to you.

New and Noteworthy is a combination of new apps and anything Apple thinks might be of interest to you. It is worth keeping an eye on this section.

In the end, while the feature page can be interesting, it is really about trendy apps. If you are primarily using the iPad for special needs, then trendy apps probably will not be what you are seeking.

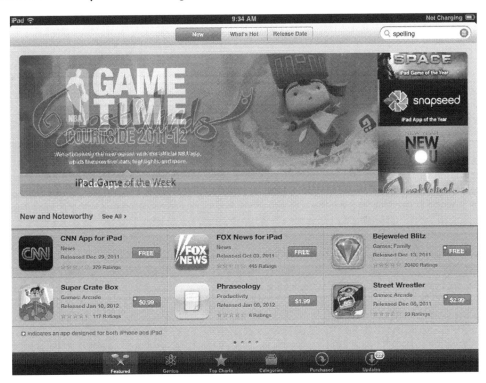

Screenshot of App Store Home Screen

Genius® Recommendations

The **Genius Recommendations** section is a very interesting feature of the App Store. Once activated, the App Store looks at the kind of apps you already have on the iPad and suggests new apps that might interest you. I have found a number of apps that have been great for Noah using this and I do suggest that you turn on the setting.

What is interesting about the Genius Recommendations is that for each recommendation, it tells you which app you already have that is prompting the new recommendation. In some cases, the newly suggested app is a companion to an app you are already using. In other cases, it may be an app within the same category, for example, Education and for approximately the same age level, complementary to an app you already have. I have located a number of really cool apps and developers I had never heard of before using the Genius Recommendation.

Screenshot of App Store Genius Recommendations

A couple of points to keep in mind:

1. The more apps you have, the more suggestions you will get
2. If you start seeing a theme of apps that you are not interested in, you can mark the **Not Interested** button at the bottom. This will tell the App Store to stop recommending apps of that type. I use this for my apps frequently, since I am really interested in finding apps for Noah or Maya.
3. Don't mark **Not Interested** if you are interested in the type of app and just not interested in a particular app. I would only mark **Not Interested** if you truly are not interested in any of the apps of that kind.
4. There are pages and pages for apps, so scroll around, tap on an app, read about

it, and if you don't like it, move on, keep looking.

Top Charts

Screenshot of App Store Top Charts

There are three lists in the Top Charts area:

1. **Top Paid Apps**
2. **Top Free Apps**
3. **Highest Grossing apps**

There is not much to say about this area, as it's pretty self-explanatory.

Categories

Each app belongs to a category in the App Store. The category to which an app belongs is determined by the developer. If you were to look at all of the apps I have for Noah on his iPad, a lot of them would categorized under education, but you would be surprised to see that some are under productivity, medical, games, and even utilities. There is actually even a special education category, but here is the thing - no one uses it. There is a lot of competition among app developers to be in the top ten of their category. There are even some developers that put their apps in certain categories just to get them to a broader audience (mainly games). So category alone is not a good way of filtering apps. That said, you can use this area to keep tabs on apps within each category. Tap on a category and you are presented with a Feature page filtered for that specific category. The page has all the same sections and ways of filtering as the main feature pages, but only for the category you are using. This is a good way to see what is happening at that moment in time for that specific category of apps.

Screenshot of App Store Categories

Purchased

Screenshot of App Store Purchased

This section allows you to see all of the apps you have purchased with the Apple ID you are using at that time. As far as Apple is concerned, a purchased app is either paid for or downloaded for free. You can sort your list in a number of ways to help you keep track of your apps.

Updates

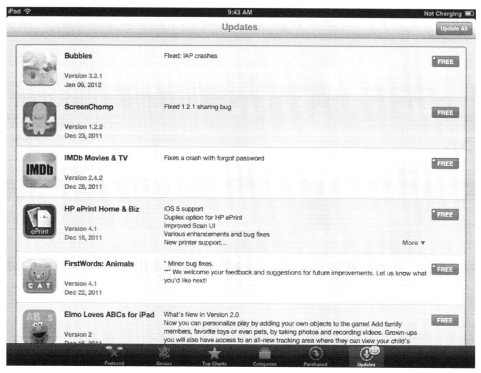

Screenshot of App Store Updates

In the update section, you will find a list of the apps currently installed on your iPad that have available updates. From this screen, you can update any app or choose to update all of them at the same time. I use this feature a lot. Note that updating your apps to the most current version does not mean you are backing up your iPad. You still need to do that independent of updating the apps on it. I see a lot of people confusing the two.

Syncing

Syncing your iPad to iTunes is the equivalent of backing up your iPad. If your computer is connected to the internet, you can also update your apps during the process, and if there is an iOS (iPad operating system) update, you can choose to update that as well. You need to sync (backup) your iPad on a regular basis. I cannot stress this enough. This is a habit you need to make into a routine.

An example to prove my point. If you are planning to use your iPad as an AAC device, you will spend hours and hours fine tuning the setup. You will also spend hours setting up other apps, video and pictures and on, and on, and on. Since the iPad is portable, the chances of something catastrophic happening to it are much higher than, let's say, a desktop computer. What happens to all of that work if something were to happen? More importantly, what happens to your user if they suddenly don't have a voice while you take the time to repurchase and rebuild? What if you don't remember all of the stuff you added or all of the detail? In short, **NOT GOOD**. Just do it!!!!

Screenshot of iTunes iPad Summary Page

There are three ways to sync your iPad:

1.   Attach the sync cable (same as the power cable) to your computer
2.   Via Wi-fi to your computer
3.   Via iCloud.

Hardwire Sync

The iPad comes with a hardwire sync cable. That same cable doubles as the power cable. Connect the USB end of the cable to your computer, connect the other end with the 30-pin docking connector to your iPad. If you have iTunes installed, which you likely do, then iTunes should launch automatically. When it does, iTunes may ask you if you want to backup your iPad. Say yes

This is the fastest way to sync your iPad. Depending on how much content you have installed on the iPad, either from downloads or taking pictures or video, and how much memory your iPad has, this can take some time, so plan for that when you first start developing the syncing habit. As it becomes part of your routine, you will know about how much time it should take.

Don't forget to check for new operating system updates regularly. This does take quite a bit of time, as it backs up, then deletes everything, then installs the new operating system, then re-installs your apps and media. It has taken me up to 20 minutes for this process and I do not keep a lot of media on my iPads.

Wi-Fi Sync

You can set up your iPad to sync automatically over your wi-fi network at home. I love this option because I don't have to create a habit of manually backing up; it just happens automatically.

You can set up wi-fi sync on the **Summary** page. On the **Summary** page in iTunes under the **Options** section, you will see a check box for **Sync with this iPad over Wi-Fi.** Select this option to enable Wi-Fi Sync. While this does not allow you to update the operating system, it does constantly keep your iPad synced with iTunes. This does not update your apps, however. You can do that update via **Update in the App Store** and then the system will automatically backup via wi-fi. The short of it is, if you have a wi-fi network, consider setting up wi-fi sync.

iCloud Sync

On the iPad summary page in iTunes you can setup iCloud sync under the **Backup Settings** section. You are making the choice whether to backup to your computer or to iCloud. You can think of iCloud as a hard drive on the internet that only you (or anyone who has your Apple ID) can access. While iCloud is free for the first 5 GB, the smallest iPad is 16 GB, meaning that most people use way more than 5 GBs of data on their iPad. As a result, you will have to pay for the upgrade in storage almost immediately.

Pros of iCloud Backup:

1. Don't need a computer to backup the iPad
2. Can backup over 3G if needed
3. Does not store apps so apps do not count agaist your total iCloud storage

Cons of iCloud Backup:

1. Need high speed internet
2. Will cost you to upgrade to enough storage to backup a whole iPad (Assuming you have lots of app data such as document and media)
3. Slower form of backup than wi-fi or hardwire
4. Restoration still requires a computer
5. If you use an slightly older version of the an app (think AAC apps) it will restore a new version and there might be conflicts in the data from version to version. While I have not seen this directly, I would plan for it. The best thing you can do is have a good plan to update the apps and backup your data.
6. Not available everywhere

CHAPTER 5

How to Get Started

Before you run out and buy an iPad, you need a plan, and you need to make sure the iPad is really going to help you meet your goals. When we first got the iPad, we did not have any specific goals, we were just going to get it and try it out. What could it hurt? I can tell you in those early days, when all my son did was lick the screen, I did not have much faith that his iPad was having any meaningful impact. And the fact is it was not. It was not until we discussed using the iPad with his teachers and therapists and started incorporating the iPad into his overall goals that we made any progress. Don't get me wrong, there are still times to this day that I catch him licking the screen, although this happens much less than before. And I still think to myself, "that isn't educational."

The message is, in short, you need to develop a plan. That plan needs to take into consideration where you are today, where you want to be both short-term and long-term, and who is available to help you get there. Addressing these three major elements is what is going to make the use of the iPad a positive. In other words, move you from aimless licking to effective tool.

Where Are You Now?

The first step in the whole process is to do a skills assessment. Noah had a number of assessments throughout the year, some by his school, others by Early Childhood Intervention (a state based early childhood program), and a third one done by an independent developmental pediatrician. It is a little bit of overkill and it will likely change over time, but Noah really did not have a solid diagnosis early on, so we explored a number of different avenues to try to help him. I suspect this is common.

Noah had an assessment shortly before he got his iPad and then another one 3 to 4 months later. In hindsight, it not only helped us get started but it also helped us, after the second assessment, really understand the impact of what we were doing.

If you don't have a current assessment, work with your therapy team, explain what you are doing and ask them to do a mini-assessment. If you are between assessments, your therapy team will know where your child is relative to their goals and what those goals are.

You are where you are, what is important is that you understand where you are. If you don't have a starting point, then you will likely fumble around getting started. The worst that happens is that your child does not engage with the iPad for whatever reason even if they are able and willing. Then you just need to retool and restart. It is not the end of the world. But it is a whole lot easier if you already know where they are and present apps that engage them at their current level. If you know where to start you can be a lot more effective.

Where Do You Want to Go? - Goals

Setting goals and coming up with a way to accomplish them is what we as special needs parents and caregivers are all about. The more I learn about my child, and the more I learn about learning and therapy, the more realistic my goals are and the better able I am to pick the most effective things on which to work. Notice, I did not use the words the right things on which to work. Effectiveness is the name of this game and in a lot of cases, this will be a life-long challenge. Frankly, therapy and learning is for everyone all of the time, it just seems more pertinent to the special needs community.

Build a Plan

Where to start? First, you need to list your goals, determining what your short-term and long-term goals are. This, of course, will be very different depending upon each individual person. If we were all the same then there would only be a handful of apps in the iTunes store, but we are not and there are not. As an example, here were our goals for Noah; I divided them into short- and long-term goals.

Short-Term Goals

Short-term goals: get engaged, interact, have some fun.

1. We wanted Noah to be able to interact with the iPad in a meaningful and purposeful way.
2. We wanted him to learn basic cause and effect to facilitate his interaction with the iPad
3. We wanted it to be fun

Things like turning the iPad on, changing apps, or other basic functionality issues were not an immediate concern for us, as we knew we would be right there to help Noah. Our real initial short-term goal was to get him interested in the device itself. One of our challenges with Noah was - and this is still kind of true today - that he really does not relate to video or other multimedia kinds of things. We were concerned at the time that with the Cerebral Palsy and sensory issues, he might not be interpreting video or multimedia in a meaningful way. As it turns out, that wasn't the issue at all. He just isn't a TV junkie like my wife, daughter, and I are. Lucky for him, really. Anyway, because of this original concern, all we really wanted to accomplish at first was a way to meaningfully engage him. Fun is a great vehicle for hard work!

How Do You Go About Creating Short-Term Goals?

Engage/Interaction/Relate/Create Value to Create Desire

When thinking about short-term goals, think about them in terms of how they can engage the user, whether that person is a child, teen, or adult. Some users will naturally gravitate to the iPad, and intuitively know how it works, what it can do, and how to interact with it. If this is the case for you, then putting your user in front of the iPad should be all you need to do. If that is not the case, however, then with a little effort, you can find something to engage them.

What will engage them? What are some things I can try?

This is where knowing your user is key. What do they like about other electronic devices or what do they like about other items in the physical world? Because the iPad can do so much, the universe of things available to you to engage your user is very broad.

Remember, the goal at this point is simply to get them excited, to get a positive reaction. With Noah, we started with colors. He was really into them at the time, so I found a color game called Toddler Teasers Color.

Noah could hit anything to start the game and it would give him a response. Selecting the wrong answer was mild in terms of response from the app, but still an event. Providing the right answer, to the contrary, cued a very dramatic and very positive response. The sticker rewards after a series of correct answers added an even greater reinforcement.

At first, Noah did not know all of his colors, all he was really doing is just hitting things on the page until a positive response happened. That was more than ok with us. We wanted the iPad to be fun for him at that point. It being an educational tools was a bonus.

What other things can I do with the iPad to engage my user?

Colors Toddler Preschool
Cost: $1
Developer: Toddler Teasers
iTunes URL: *http://itunes.apple.com/us/app/colors-toddler-preschool/id303146526?mt=8*

The premise of the app is simple, it presents a selection of colors to the user in a variety of settings and asks them pick a particular one. Pick the right one and you get applause, and the color spins, twirls, etc. Correctly pick a certain number in a row, and it gives you a sticker that you can then digitally stick to a page. As you progress, you will collect more stickers. If you select the wrong color, it will say something like, "*awww, pick again,*" and the wrong answer is removed, leaving you with the rest of the options. It will dwindle down to the last answer. Then, after so many correct answers, you can pick a sticker.

Screenshot of Colors Toddler Preschool

Sound Touch
Cost: $4
Developer:
iTunes URL: *http://itunes.apple.com/us/app/sound-touch/id348094440?mt=8*

This is a great interactive getting started app. Within the app there are pages around different themes, for example, music or small animals. Tap on a page and the user is presented with a 3 by 4 grid of different icons. Tap on a particular animal icon, and a full page picture of the animal appears and the sound made by that animal is then played. Tap again to go back to the screen with the grid. Tap a second time on the same icon and get a different picture of the same animal and a second sound, and so forth and so on. Each icon has 4 different pictures and 4 different sounds. It can teach the user very rapidly that an animal is not a picture of a particular animal but that the picture is a concept of a kind of animal. I am sure there is a fancy learning team for this, but for me, the fact that it helps the learner get to the concepts behind an animal versus a literal picture provides a lot of cognitive development in one shot.

Screenshot of Sound Touch

Games

One of the very first places to start is simple interactive games. As compared to video arcade games, these simple interactive games seem almost one-dimensional. But what they lack in dimension can be used to your advantage. The adage that the simplest things in life are the best is very true in this case.

What to Look for in Simple Interactive Games:

What to look for in simple interactive games:

1. Simple to use and understand
2. 1 or 2 dimensions to the game
3. If the game has more than 2 instructions, it is likely not a good candidate for starting
4. It should be intuitive to use
5. If it is subtle, make sure it is not too subtle for your user
6. Conversely, if it is over the top, make sure it is not too over the top for your user.

 ### Bubbles
Cost: $1
Developer: Hog Bay Software
iTunes URL: *http://itunes.apple.com/us/app/bubbles/id284288607?mt=8*

Bubbles is just that, run your hand across screen once and you create a line of bubbles. Tap on a bubble and it pops. Just like in real life, making bubbles and popping them is very addictive. I will tell you that my wife and I both can still to this day be caught creating and popping bubbles.

Screenshot of Bubbles

Bubble Wrap

Cost: $1
Developer: Lima Sky
iTunes URL: *http://itunes.apple.com/us/app/bubble-wrap/id409695793?mt=8*

Just like popping bubble wrap in real life, the digital version can be just as addictive. The digital version has different sized bubbles. This is important for those physically challenged and younger users, as they may be better able to hit a larger ta

Screenshot of Bubble Wrap

Letters and Numbers

Letters or numbers may also be of interest to your user and allow them to get engaged. That was the case with Noah early on. He did not know any of the letters or numbers before he started using the iPad, but trying to guess the right answer was very interesting to him, so he ended up learning both really quickly just to get praise from the game.

Interactive Alphabet
Cost: $3
Developer: ABC Flash Cards
iTunes URL: *http://itunes.apple.com/us/app/interactive-alphabet-abc-flash/*

id383967580?mt=8

Interactive Alphabet is a very simple and interesting way to present the alphabet. Every letter gets its own page, there are lots of items on each page to interact with and a number of hidden and self-referential items to uncover and find. Very engaging for all levels. There is even a very young child mode that just plays the whole alphabet rather than requiring the user to tap to move the program forward.

Screenshot of Interactive Alphabet

Numbers Toddler Preschool
Cost: $1
Developer: Toddler Teasers
iTunes URL: *http://itunes.apple.com/us/app/numbers-toddler-preschool/id303149530?mt=8*

Numbers Toddler Preschool starts with 3 numbers on a page from 1 to 10 and asks you to pick a specific number. When you tap the correct answer, it responds with applause. If you tap an incorrect answer, you are asked to try again until you get it right. There are options to increase the choices between 1 and 100. After so many correct answers you can pick a sticker.

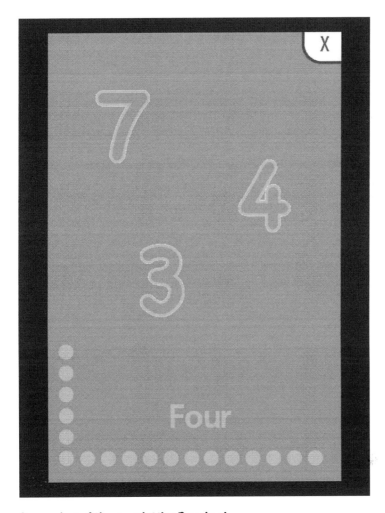

Screenshot of Number Toddler Preschool

Video

Video can be a wonderful way to engage your user. If they already have a portable player or if they respond well to TV or video, then playing video on the iPad can be great way to introduce them to the iPad.

For a user who is old enough to and can operate the iPad, you can let them freely explore the video sites and their content. While it took Noah a while to understand how to navigate the various channels and ages groups, I have been amazed by some of the content that he likes. For example, there is one he has found that is from "America Funniest Home Videos" of a baby sucking on a lemon. He loves it, it just tickles his funny bone.

Kids Videos and Entertainment – Kideos

Cost: $3

Developer: Big Purple Hippos

iTunes URL: *http://itunes.apple.com/us/app/kids-videos-entertainment/id348733245?mt=8*

Kideos is website that has all sorts of YouTube videos broken down by age group (from 0-2, 2-4, etc) that have all been screened and categorized so as to remove inappropriate content either by the description of that content or by age. Kideos then went on to develop an iPad application.

Screenshot of Kids Videos and Entertainment - Kideos

Apple Video App

Cost: Included with iPad

Developer: Apple

iTunes URL: *http://www.apple.com/ipad/built-in-apps/mail.html*

The Video app on the iPad is used in conjunction with the iTunes application on your PC. You can either buy or download video content into iTunes and then copy the video to the iPad by syncing it with iTunes. The advantage to using the Video app is that you can control the exact content the user sees and can access. I have seen a number of parents download home movies to or shoot home movies right on the iPad. Home movies can be comforting, provide a point of reference, and they can be used to preview an upcoming activity (such as getting a hair cut).

Screenshot of Apple Video App

Music

Music has long been used in both therapy and as entertainment, so it makes sense to use it as a way to introduce the iPad. A favorite piece of music can be used to bring the user's attention to the iPad. Because music can be so important to your special needs user, the iPad can also become their primary iPod (i.e., the primary place where they keep their music and the primary device they use to play it). While the iPad is certainly not as portable as an iPod Touch or iPod, the larger interface can be a great alternative to nothing at all.

Remember, licking the iPad is not educational. But for almost any child, a drum kit can be a lot of fun. For a child with physical challenges, banging out a riff on a drum or doing a drum roll can be a lot of fun.

A word of caution, though. For those with sensory issues, this can also be a negative experience. Noah had a number of sensory issues, so when we first started with an app, he would often let us know if they were too much for him by saying the words, "no, no..." and hitting the home button to change the app. Sometimes, we could identify the ones that would be problematic in advance, but sometimes not. His is a very obvious response. There are many more subtle responses, though, so when you start, keep an eye out for changes in behavior. We have found that as he has gotten older and developed more, Noah is better able to handle more sensory apps, including ones that we would have sworn a year ago he would never use. It just goes to show, your child can always surprise you. But this makes sense. We have done a lot of experimenting. Some of the experiments work, some don't, and some apps we experiment with are more advanced or "not the thing" Noah needs right now. Remember though, what is not the thing now may be the thing later.

Finger Drums!

Cost: Free
Developer: Indigo Penguin Limited
iTunes URL: *http://itunes.apple.com/us/app/finger-drums!/id407511090?mt=8*

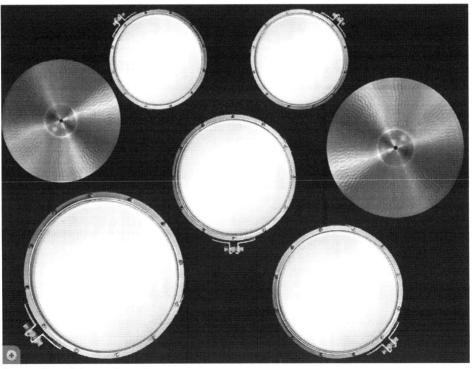

Screenshot of Finger Drums!

Finger Drums App Breakout: You will locate a number of apps when you search for Finger Drums, but the premise is the same for all. There is a drum kit, with various drums arranged in a semi circle so that one hand can play the drums. As you can imagine, hitting the cymbal or tom drum is a lot of fun. You can also imagine that hitting the cymbal a hundred times in a row may not be as much fun for you.

Magic Piano HD

Cost: $2
Developer: Smule
iTunes URL: http://itunes.apple.com/us/app/magic-piano-hd/id356416346?mt=8

This is a very fun interactive piano program. There are a number of creative ways to make music not only with the piano but also just by tapping on the screen.

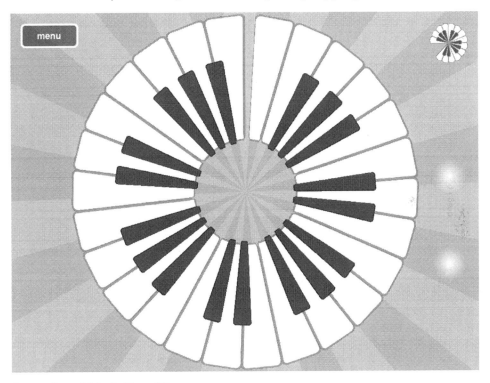

Screenshot of Magic Piano HD

Drawing

Drawing apps can also be a draw, no bad pun intended. They allow the user to interact and have a direct response with the iPad. This can be something as simple as drawing a line, or more complex, such as coloring in an object.

Spawn Illuminati HD

Cost: $1
Developer: Elements of Design LLC
iTunes URL: *http://itunes.apple.com/us/app/spawn-illuminati-hd-art-fireworks/id296036692?mt=8*

This is a very visually intense application. The app starts out with swirling lines that have a life of their own. They swirl and swirl around the screen, bouncing off the sides of the iPad. When you draw your hand across or touch any part of the screen the swirls will react to your touch.

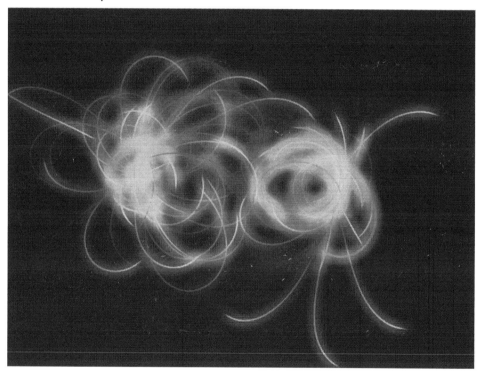

Screenshot of Spawn Illuminati HD

Magic Ink

Cost: $2
Developer: qarl
iTunes URL: *http://itunes.apple.com/us/app/magic-ink/id382113288?mt=8*

Magic Ink App Breakout: Magic Ink is a drawing program that takes full advantage of the sensors on the screen of the iPad. The more pressure you apply to the surface as you draw, the thicker the line. When you draw, it will smooth out your strokes in such a way as to make almost anything you draw look fluid. Each line will only stay on the screen for a limited amount of time. It is safe to say that everything you do is fluid and temporary. This makes it a perfect introductory application to the iPad. You can create something nice, but because it only lasts a little while, you find yourself wanting to create more.

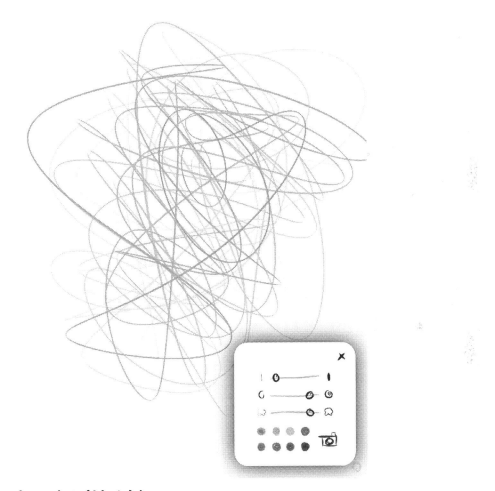

Screenshot of Magic Ink

Learnl Finger Paint

Cost: $2
Developer: Orange Design, Inc.
iTunes URL: *http://itunes.apple.com/us/app/learnl-finger-paint/id364464406?mt=8*

Finger Paint (Learnl) app Breakout: Finger Paint is a drawing program; you can select from a number of different animals that you can then color in, similar to a coloring book. You can shake the iPad and the animal will make the appropriate sound and move around a little. You can also take a picture of your drawing at any point. The pictures are then stored in the iPad's photo album. Beware, though. Both of my kids like the picture button and the noise it makes, so at any any given moment there are hundreds of pictures of the same animal in various stages of color.

Screenshot of Learnl (original artwork by one of my kids)

Long-Term Goals

Once we knew Noah was hooked on the iPad, we started looking for ways we could incorporate use of the iPad into his goals. The first place we started was with Noah's teachers and his therapists. We discussed his goals both academically and therapeutically, and then tried to find ways at home to reinforce those goals, either through finding new software or repurposing current software. Just like everything else in Noah's life, we tried to disguise therapy as fun.

We took the goals he was working on in class and adapted them to the iPad where appropriate. For example, when it comes to writing letters, Noah uses an adapted pen; we also use an adapted stylus with the iPad. In fact, we brought a number of styluses to the school and asked that they help us select the right one and adapt it in the best manner. It is important to keep in mind that not all therapy is suited for the virtual world of the iPad, and to not force the wrong type of therapy or activities to be on the iPad. An iPad is just like anything else, it is only one tool amongst many. It is very easy to get caught up in an iPad only solution.

Our Story With the School

When we got Noah's iPad, his then-teacher was not very familiar with AAC devices or other Assistive Technology. Granted, it was the 2 year old class and it was very hands on in the room. Lots of art work would come home for the fridge. At the time, Noah was just starting to get the hang of the iPad. Looking back and knowing what we know now, we could have gotten him more able with it much faster, but at the time we were only one of 2 students in the school who had an iPad, and the other student was much older.

Noah attends a special needs school, so, generally speaking, the teachers were very familiar with accommodating "extra gear." Noah soon moved into a new class with older students. He was about 2 and half at the time. We were very fortunate that his new teacher was very experienced with AAC devices and how to get the students using them, as well as how to incorporate them in the classroom. She was so good at it that we realized how much more he could get out of the program if she was more familiar with the technology. We helped her get an iPad for her class and also helped the head teacher of the school get an iPad. We felt that it was important to have the head teacher also have first hand experience with the technology. It turned out that both teachers had such a strong response in their classroom that the teachers used money from their own fund raiser to buy an iPad for every classroom in the school. Big move for a small underfunded school.

Getting iPads into Schools

We were very lucky in a lot of ways when it comes to our experience with Noah's school. Being a special needs school, they were very open to accommodating new technology. We were also lucky in the sense that even though his teacher did not have an iPad, she was very familiar with AAC devices and technology. The challenge was how to implement a technology when we did not really know what we were doing, they (i.e., the school) did not know what they were doing, and none of us were really sure if it was going to work.

I realized pretty quickly that getting his teacher to not only use it but use it effectively was the key. I went to the school knowing that they did not have the money to invest in unproven technology. This is the case everywhere, so what I needed to do was find a way to prove it to them. I went back to my wife and got permission to buy a second iPad to give to his teacher. I realize for a lot of people this is just not an option; the good news is that increasingly the iPad is being recognized as an exceptional educational tool and is being funded by more and more groups, including a lot of schools. At the time, we took a gamble and it paid off. Within a few months of working with the teacher, the rest of the teachers and the school did a fund raiser and bought an iPad for each classroom. We now had momentum.

Why is momentum important? Having the iPad in the classroom is not going to do your child much good if the people teaching them are not incorporating it into their lesson plans and into skill-building. I wanted to see two things happen. First, we were going through all of these assessments to determine what skills we needed to focus on, and I wanted to use the iPad in the classroom to help reinforce this skill-building. Second, I wanted to work on skill-building at home, and if I could get the school and his teacher on board with the iPad, I could do all of that reinforcement at home using it, since I don't have all of their other therapy, skill-building items, or tools in my house. And I guess there is another thing: I really want to them to teach me. The iPad ended up being a learning experience for all of us.

As our collective experience grew, we started to see other kids with iPads in the class, the class itself got more iPads, and soon we were doing exactly what I hoped we could do, which was surround Noah with a comprehensive therapy strategy with each group doing their part, and everyone working towards a common goal. A reoccurring theme throughout this entire experience is that Laura and I play the role of orchestra conductor in Noah's life. When we can get all of the members of the band - and because of Noah's issues we have a big band - to play together and every once in a while in key, we get an enormous amount done, with huge leaps forward. But when the band is not all playing from the same sheet music, it's discordant. Of course, the iPad is only one part of this.

Lessons Learned:

1. Technology without a direction is useless
2. Lots of hand holding is needed to implement any new technology
3. Help the school come up with a long-term technology strategy, for example, backups, buyings apps, sharing lessons learned, etc.
4. Administrators need to be on board
5. Sharing amongst teachers and parents is critical

Our Story With His Therapists

For a number of reasons, since Noah started using the iPad we have gone through 3 physical therapists (PTs), 3 occupational therapists (OTs), 1 cognitive developmental therapist, and we have tried to get him speech therapy three separate times. So we can't really comment on his use of it with a speech therapist, which, of course, would be one of the best uses of the iPad. At any rate, when it came to PT, we did not see much use of the iPad as a motivator. We just did not need it. I have heard a number of stories both from parents and PTs about how they use the iPad as a motivator, though. I have heard of it used on treadmills for exercises and for potty training.

When it came to OT, we had a mixed experience. We used the iPad a lot for Fine Motor Development. We have used it to develop finger isolation and pincher grip. When we first started with the iPad, Noah's hands were in a fist most of the time. Now, a year and half later, his hands are open most of the time. I am not saying it is all the iPad, because it is not. What I am saying is that through gaming, play, learning and other interactive applications, the iPad has been a real motivator for getting him to open his hands. Why? Because it is easier to play games with a pointer finger rather than the edge of your fist. Again, without a lot of occupational therapy, we would not be here. I am just saying the iPad provided a lot of motivation to do the therapy.

Where the iPad really was outstanding was with our cognitive developmental therapist. That's where he had real leaps forward. She also was the person who recommended that we get the iPad in the first place, so she was the one who started the whole thing for us and found a ton of different ways to use the iPad to engage him. We found a lot of games and apps that Noah found entertaining. As he learned more, we then found ourselves having to find more apps, and so on and so on. It builds on itself.

Our real lessons learned both with the iPad, and I would also say, in general, were that the real value of therapy is not the one hour a week that Noah gets of any specific therapy. It is that we learned really early on to reinforce whatever skills he needs to work on and incorporate them into as many daily events as possible. Here is were the iPad can really shine; it can disguise therapy as fun. In other words, what we were doing was to turn one hour of concentrated therapy per week into therapy all of the time, using the iPad as a platform for many different kinds of therapy, and deliver that same therapy in many different ways. Again, disguising therapy as fun.

Monkey Preschool Lunchbox

Cost: $1
Developer: THUP Games
iTunes URL: *http://itunes.apple.com/us/app/monkey-preschool-lunchbox/id328205875?mt=8*

This app has a series of seven games for kids ages 2 - 5 years old. There are simple memory pages, puzzles, matching, counting, letters and numbers. After so many in a row you get to pick a sticker. Lots of fun and very interactive.

Screenshot of Monkey Preschool Lunchbox

Letters Toddler Preschool

Cost: $1
Developer: Toddler Teasers
iTunes URL: *http://itunes.apple.com/us/app/letters-toddler-preschool/id303150145?mt=8*

Letters Toddler Preschool starts you off by picking the correct letter in a field of 4 letters; it then moves up to a field of 6. If you pick the correct letter, it applauds; if you pick the wrong letter, it lets you off gently and has you try again. After so many correct answers you can pick a sticker.

Screenshot of Letters Toddler Preschool

What Do You Need to Get There? - Skills and People

Skills

Skills are where the rubber meets the road. All large tasks, all goals are broken down into skills. There are different progressions of the these tasks depending upon what model you are working with, but they all generally follow the same path. For people with special needs, all of life may be broken down into skills that need to be mastered. The iPad is a great tool for building and reinforcing some of these skills.

Nurses think in medical skills, therapists think in physical skills and educators think in academic skills. Because of this, as parents we are constantly attempting to manage skills of one sort or another. For us, our first skills started in the hospital and we have been managing an ever-increasing number of them ever since. For the most part, we have fallen into the rhythm of meeting with a therapist, doctor or teacher, listening to their assessment, then later talking between ourselves and then comparing what we have just heard to what we already knew. Some things make the cut of our stack-ranked priority list, some things get re-prioritized, and others do not make it on our list.

The iPad became really effective for us when we took Noah's assessment from his behavioral pediatrician and applied it to his IEP or Individual Educational Plan at school. We were fortunate that Noah's school used a special needs curriculum called the Carolina Curriculum, which breaks down all of his goals in 6 major categories into specific skills. Because of this, we were able to isolate specific skills that were lacking, as well as those that were not. After his next assessment, we were able to determine which he had mastered and which goals needed further work. We used both his teachers and his developmental pediatrician to help us understand where he needed to go and in what order.

 Key Point: One of the really challenging things about special needs is that not only is every child different, but in any given category or skill, they can be ahead in some aspects and behind in others. Skill priority order for one child likely will not match that of another child. It is very important that you work with all of your available resources to understand and validate the skill priority order in your plan and constantly monitor and adjust it as you go along. I say this because there have been many times where my instincts have told me that Noah needs to work on X set of skills only to have his doctors, therapists or teachers explain that Y set is much better at this time and why.

Skill priority order is hard for a lot of reasons:

1. As parents, we are not professionals, we don't necessarily understand all of the research or the current thinking
2. "Typical" does not apply to our special needs kids
3. Because your kid likely has a mixed set of skills, what comes next is not always what comes next.

That said, you as the parent know more about your child than anyone, all of the training in the world only gets you half of the equation. Your child is the other half. Your instincts will drive a lot of your decisions. My advice when planning your skill priorities:

1. Use as much of your resource network as possible when developing your plan
2. Get lots of advice, from teachers, therapists, and other parents
3. Create a feedback loop between yourself and the caregivers, therapists, teachers, etc. - make sure they understand what you are doing and ask them if they can see it working,
4. Be open to what seems like counter-intuitive skill order
5. Experiment - find out what works, be prepared to try new things if it does not
6. Always be ready to readjust your skill list
7. Always be ready to readjust your skill list (I know I said it twice, it is that important)

iPad as Management Tool

As a side note, the iPad can be used as a management tool as well. Early on we were given some really brilliant advice. We were told to keep everything in a binder or calendar. In it we should keep his discharge summary, his immunization records, and key contacts. We decided to go with an organizer which has a calendar, contacts and records in the book. In the organizer, we do things like record events, appointments, and weight, and we do it for both kids. The paper format works well for us, but we also use an electronic calendar to manage all of our scheduling, as it is the most up to date, and use the organizer just to document the decision after the fact.

If you want to use the iPad as a management device, there are a few programs you can use. If you do, make sure you think through who will get to use it and when. For example, if you are using the iPad primarily as a device for communication, you would not want to take it out of your child's hands while they are talking to someone just so you can look something up or make an appointment.

 Important Note: Going digital can be great, it can mean that you can access information anywhere at any time, so long as you have an internet connection. Think this through, though. There have been some times where we have not had an internet connection, so having the information in paper form has been best for us. There have been other times where we have forgotten our organizer and have had a problem. So it goes both ways. My advice is to just think it through.

 ## Apple Calendar
Cost: Free
Developer: Apple Inc.
iTunes URL: *http://www.apple.com/ipad/built-in-apps/mail.html*

iCal® is the default calendar application on the iPad and can sync with any of the calendar formats and systems the iPad supports. Laura and I use shared Google calendars to help manage our busy schedules, the kids' events and all appointments. We have a calendar for each person in the family and have it set up to sync to our office Outlook, our phones and my iPad. It all syncs online, so we are are always up to date when adding new things to the calendar.

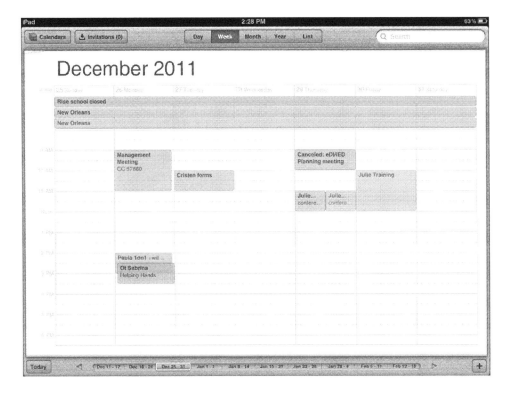

Screenshot of Apple Calendar

Apple Mail
Cost: Free
Developer: Apple
iTunes URL: *http://www.apple.com/ipad/built-in-apps/mail.html*

iMail® is Apple's email client. It is very simple and allows you to have multiple email boxes at once. The iPad and the mail client are ideally suited for reading lots of email, but it admittedly can be difficult to respond to email on the iPad using the virtual keyboard.

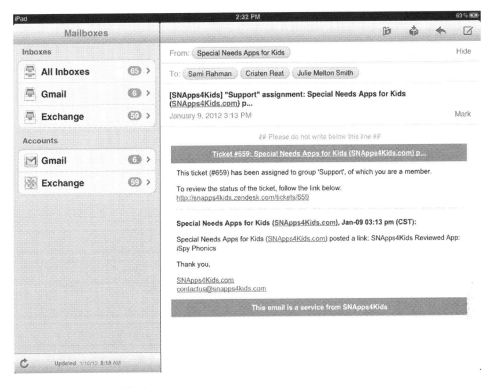

Screenshot of Apple Mail

IEP Checklist

Cost: Free
Developer: Nurvee LLC
iTunes URL: *http://itunes.apple.com/us/app/iep-checklist/id348702423?mt=8*

This is a IEP Checklist program that helps you manage the IEP process. You can create a number of IEPs and keep very detailed notes under each section and sub-section of the IEP. It is based around federal guidelines for IEPs.

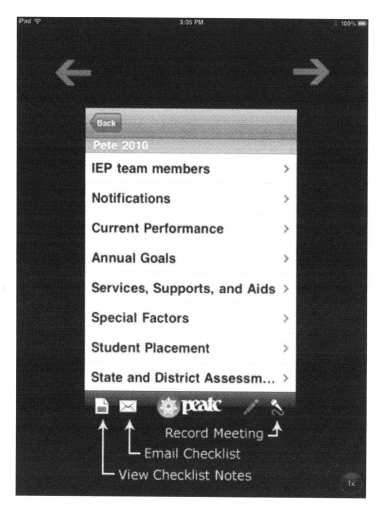

Screenshot of IEP Checklist

Springpad

Cost: Free
Developer: Spring Partners
iTunes URL: *http://itunes.apple.com/us/app/springpad/id360116898?mt=8*

Springpad is like a notebook that is online, on your phone and on your iPad. Whenever I need to keep notes about something, research a product I want to buy, or come across an article on the internet I want to save for later, I create a folder in Springpad and clip the webpage or add a note or a to-do. It then syncs this information and makes it available in all of my devices so I always have it.

Screenshot of Springpad

Who Can Help You Get There?

It is important to do this as a team. You need to get the school, the therapists and your caregivers all on the same page. If you can accomplish this, you will effectively be providing a form of therapy nearly every time you use the iPad.
Caregiver

From the caregiver perspective, the iPad can often be perceived as being a toy or just for entertainment purposes. And, in many ways, it can be and is. But if you spend some time with your caregivers and educate them as to how to use the iPad so they are comfortable, and more importantly on how you are using the iPad as a therapeutic or educational tool, and really show them how you are using it and how your child uses it, what to look for, and what to watch out for, the iPad can be used effectively even when you are not around.
Therapists

You will undoubtably have some therapists who embrace this technology and others who will not. This is the case with adoption rates for all technology. Your therapy team can be your biggest allies and resource pool, so it is important that you approach each member, get their feedback, understand where they are coming from, and help them see where you want to go. In general, even before the iPad came into our lives, I spent a lot of time with Noah's therapists understanding how they work, how they think and what is important to them. Noah started getting therapy before we even left the hospital, so the contacts we made there helped us make the transition from the hospital - a medical environment - to the outside world before he even started attending school. They were our first group of experts, so I wanted to learn as much as I could from them. I think we have been very lucky and in general have had lots of great, energetic and enthusiastic people on our team. I understand that is not always the case. Here is my point: if you have the resources available to you, try your best to utilize them.

Utilizing this resource can come in a number of different forms. For example, I use my son's therapy team to help me understand the steps necessary to get to a particular goal. Some of those steps may have nothing to do with the iPad and often are conversations that don't even reference the iPad. Other times, I use our resources to help me directly develop exercises with the iPad.
Educators and Schools

The school your child attends can and should be a major resource for both information and experimentation. We have used the assessments we receive at the beginning of each year to map the skills we want to focus on that year. During our meeting with the school, we make a case for our goals for Noah and help set them in his plan. We also use daily and weekly feedback to help reinforce school goals at home. For example, word usage, letter of the week, numbers, math and penmanship are all incorporated into Noah's goals. We then take these short-term goals and reinforce them at home using the iPad.

Like his therapists, we use Noah's special education teachers to help us understand how to develop goals and implement both short-term and long-term goals. We've been very lucky to have come across a number of teachers and administrators who have significant experience dealing with special needs and assistive technology, both high- and low-tech versions.

Checklists

Getting Started Check List :

1. What are my overall goals?

    - Use the iPad as a:

        - Communication Device

        - Educational Device

        - Therapy Device

        - Life-skills Management Device

        - Entertainment Device

        - Or None of the Above

2. What are my short-term goals?
3. What are my long-term goals
4. Who needs to be involved or brought into the process?

    - Teachers

    - Therapists

    - Doctors

    - Caregivers

CHAPTER 6

iPad Setup: What You Really Need to Know

The good news is that there are a lot of ways you can customize the user experience on the iPad. The bad news is that you need to go through all of the options to determine which ones are important to you and the ultimate user.

In a nut shell, there are three major areas you need to decide how you want to handle. The first is preferences: volume, screen rotation, what certain buttons do, backdrop, login image. For some users, this will be very important and they will want them set up very carefully; for others, it may not matter and they may want the user to set it up themselves or use the default settings.

The second major area of setup is access control: can you access the internet, can you delete apps, add apps, buy apps, download content from iTunes, can you share stuff with other people? This is a very broad topic that has a lot of potential pitfalls that we will walk through, but the key is that the default settings on a iPad do not restrict much of anything, including any adult content, so you need to make some basic decisions. Making no decision at all is a bad way to go.

Preferences

In the preference section, you will deal with

1. Managing Volume
2. Brightness
3. Managing Screen Rotation
4. Side Switch Preference: Mute or Rotation
5. Backdrop and Login screen graphics

Volume

Once your child learns where the volume rocker is, you will most likely be forever turning the volume down on the iPad. The good news is that, like the iPods, you can set a limit to the volume of the headphone jack, so if your child uses headphones they will not do permanent damage to their ear drums. The not so great news is that there is no method to limit the volume of the external speaker. In most cases, this may not be an issue. There are some times, however, with some media like video, where the audio is boosted and that can be very loud. I have yet to find software to limit the speaker volume across the board, so what I have below are tricks you can use.

Managing Volume

How to manage volume without software is a good question, and the answer will depend upon what thing's volume you are trying to control. Keep in mind that this section is for when your child knows how to control the volume and always turns it up to the highest level and the volume is too loud. In many cases, you will have the exact opposite problem and will need/want a speaker to boost the volume.

For media, including audio files such as music and video:

1. Control the media volume when creating it. If you are creating your own media, such as making video or converting videos for use on the iPad, you can adjust the master volume at the time of creation. If you find that the volume is consistently loud or is distorted, then it is likely that the conversion software is boosting the audio. This may also be adjustable. If you are converting audio from CD or some other source, there should also be a way to deal with the master volume during the conversion process. How to do this will differ from software to software.

2. If you are using commercial media, such as videos or music from iTunes, you will find that in most cases volume cannot be boosted so much that it is too loud. That said, movies are getting louder and louder with things like special effects and explosions. Also, music videos can be loud. Muffling the volume may be your only solution to this issue (See section below).

For Applications

Most application volume levels are not too loud, however, you will come across some that are. Since the applications rely on the operating system to manage volume, they don't typically provide you a method to control the master volume. If the app has a master volume control, use it. Most will not, in which case you will be left with muffling the volume mechanically.

How to Muffle the Volume Mechanically:

1. Cases: Some iPad cases will naturally muffle the volume, particularly where the case offers a lot of protection or is designed to be sealed
2. Block the speaker: Use tape over the speaker. Taping it completely will usually muffle the sound too much, so I would make sure there is a hole in the tape. The advantage of tape is that you can remove and replace it as needed without a lot of cost.

Controlling Volume Electronically

There are a number of ways to control the volume of an app electronically on the iPad.

Volume Control in General Settings

In the **Settings** app, under the general section, you will find the Sounds preferences. When you click on **Sounds,** it will give you a volume slider; slide left to reduce the volume, slide right to increase the volume. These settings are only temporary and act like an overall sound booster or governor. In other words, if you use any other method to change the volume and then come back to this section, you will see that the volume slider only reflects the current volume level.

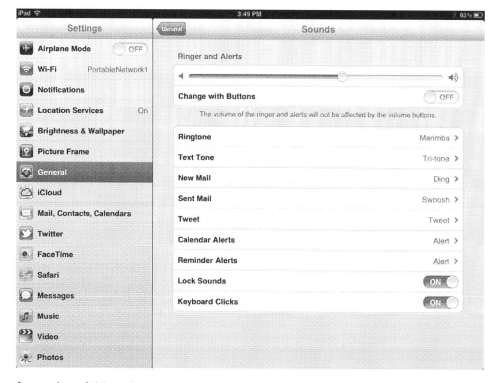

Screenshot of Volume Control in General Settings

Headphone volume control

In the **Settings** app, under the Music tab, select **Volume Limit.** The default setting is turned off. Turning it on and adjusting the volume slider will limit (govern) the maximum volume that the headphone jack will produce. This is a very good idea for someone who uses the headphones, especially one who knows how to control the volume and has a tendency to crank the volume to the max. The idea behind this feature is to prevent hearing loss, and it is a good feature. I wish they had extended it to the external speaker.

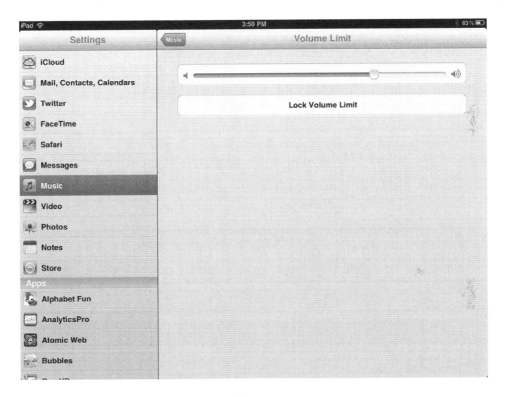

Screenshot of Headphone Volume Control Settings

Media volume control

Volume control when playing video

When you are playing any video using the built-in video player - video in the Video App or video from the internet, as an example - the video player has a volume slider just above/below the play/pause button. Slide it to the left to reduce the volume, slide to the right to increase the volume.

Screenshot of Volume Slider in the Video App

Volume control when playing audio files

The iPod app has a volume slider in the upper left hand corner above the Play/Pause button. Slide to the left and the volume will decrease, slide to the right and the volume will increase.

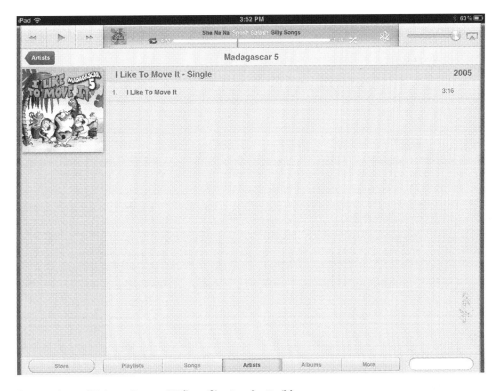

Screenshot of Volume Control When Playing Audio Files:

Controlling Volume Physically

Volume Rocker

This volume rocker on the outside of the iPad can allow you to control the master volume of the iPad itself. Press the top of the rocker and the volume will go up, press the lower part of the rocker and the volume will go down. Press and hold on the lower button and the iPad will instantly go to no volume at all, effectively putting the iPad into mute node.

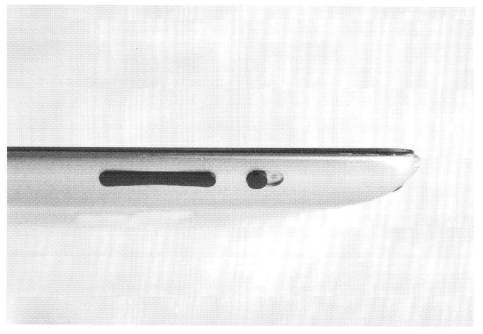

iPad 2 Volume Rocker and Slider (mute or rotate depending on settings)

Slider Set to Mute Mode

The default mode of the slider above the volume rocker is to put the iPad into Mute Mode (i.e., no volume from any source, media, audio or application).

Headphones

Some headphones have both an audio signal booster and limiter built into them. This allows you to adjust the volume of any signal coming into the headphones from any device. You might get the same effect from limiting the volume of the headphones electronically in the settings section of the iPad.

Tape

Tape can be put over the speaker holes on both the iPad 1 and 2. I would recommend against completely covering the speaker, as this will likely reduce the overall volume too much. You can either partially cover the holes or put holes in the tape before you install it on the iPad. I would NOT recommend adding the tape and then trying to poke holes in it once it is installed. Particularly for the iPad 1, you could permanently damage the speaker if you slip up or go too far.

Case

The iPad case itself can muffle the volume of the speaker by the nature of its design, particularly those cases that are designed to seal the iPad from the outside world. The more protective the case, the more it will likely muffle the volume of the speaker. Keep this in mind as most people will have the opposite problem and want the speaker to be louder or may even want to add an external speaker.

Brightness

The screen brightness can be adjusted manually or automatically, or a combination of both. The brighter the screen, the more power the iPad consumes. Also, if the screen is either too bright or not bright enough, you may be creating conditions that will increase eye strain.

Auto-Brightness

The iPad has a light sensor right above the camera on the iPad 2 and above the screen in the same location on the iPad 1. The idea behind the sensor is that the iPad will adjust the screen brightness automatically, based on the lighting conditions it detects through its sensor. This of course only works if the the auto-brightness setting is turned on.

Adjusting Brightness

How to adjust the brightness of the screen:

1. In the settings program, tap on **Brightness & Wallpaper**
2. Default settings

   - Brightness at 50%

   - Auto-Brightness turned on

3. If you want to increase the brightness of the screen, move the brightness slider to the right, to decrease move to the left

   - I find the default value of 50% to not be bright enough so I normally have mine set at 60% or so. I have not noticed any decrease in battery life at this setting

4. Auto-Brightness: I would recommend keeping it on.

   - I think it is great when I open my iPad while in a dark room, and it quickly adjusts the screen to a much lower brightness level, for example, when I can't sleep and I want to read in bed.

   - There are times when I want the brightness to be a certain way, so I just adjust the setting accordingly and readjust when I don't need those settings anymore.

Background Image and Login Image

This may not seem like much of a feature or anything to focus on with a special needs user, but I have found that most special needs users have an image of a particular person on their iPad. Most of them either have a parent, a sibling, an image of themselves or of something very important to them, like a toy or a pet. Most of us enjoy customizing objects in our lives for ourselves, and I think changing the background and login image on the iPad is a simple yet powerful way to connect the user to the device.

Before you start, you want to make sure that the image you want is in the photo app already and looks the way you want it to look. To change the background and login image:

1. In the **Settings** application, tap on **Brightness & Wallpaper**
2. Tap under the words **Wallpaper** on either of the two iPad images,
3. You will be presented with two options

    - **Wallpaper** to select from the list of built-in wallpapers

    - **Camera Roll** to pick an image from the Photo application. Since we are customizing it with a personal picture, select **Camera Roll**

4. Scroll through the list of images until you find the one you want to use and tap on it.
5. The screen will change, and you will now see the image at full size and see a tool bar along the top
6. The tool bar has the following options:

    - **Cancel** to go back

    - **Set Lock Screen** - this will set the image as the login image

    - **Set Home Screen** - this will set the image as the wallpaper on the Home screen

    - **Set Both** - this will set the image to both Login Screen and wallpaper of Home screen

Screen Rotation Button vs Mute Button Slider and Alternatives

Above the volume rocker there is a programable slider. Originally, this slider controlled the rotation lock setting. If the slider is open (or unlocked), using its built-in Accelerometer sensor, the iPad attempts to sense the orientation of the screen - either landscape or portrait - and rotates the screen automatically to match the iPad's orientation. Flip the iPad from one orientation to the next and it will adjust automatically. This is a very cool feature most of the time. However, with special needs users, depending on their mobility and how the iPad is positioned, this can sometimes cause the iPad to rotate uncontrollably between orientations, and most importantly, undesirably. As a solution to this problem, setting the slider to the closed (locked) position will disable the auto rotation feature and keep the screen in whatever position it was locked into until it is unlocked again. At some point in the first year, an operating system upgrade changed the slider from rotation lock to mute/unmute. Then a subsequent update gave you the ability to select which of the two functions you wanted to use the slider to control.

First, let's talk about what feature you might want to want to have activated by the slider and then how you would access and trigger the other feature.

Selecting which feature to control with the slider:

1. In the **Settings** application, tap on **General**
2. Tap **Use Slide Switch To**

    *   Lock Rotation

    *   Mute - Default

3.   Select the one you want.

In most cases, I would recommend changing the slider to **Lock Rotation**. If mute is more important or you use it more than lock rotation, you can always use the media control panel in the Multitasking User interface to control the screen rotation.

Multitasking User Interface

The multitasking user interface has two primary purposes:

1. Allows you to switch between any applications that have been launched and also shutdown an app already launched
2. Allows you to manage frequently used media settings on the iPad. You can control:

    *   Screen rotation lock

    *   Brightness

    *   Play, jump to the beginning and jump to the end of a song in music app

    *   Volume control

    *   Button to launch iTunes library of media

Accessing the Multitasking User Interface

Accessing the Multitasking user interface can be done either in an application or on the home screen.

To Manage Apps:

1. Double tap the home button, and the dock and the whole screen will rise to reveal the multitasking user interface.

   - You will see icons of the all the apps that have been started on the iPad; the first app on the left will be last used app and so on down the line.

2. Touch and slide your finger to the left to reveal more apps, keep sliding till you get to the end.

Screenshot of Apps in Multitasking User Interface

To Manage Media settings:

1. Double tap the home button, the dock and the whole screen will rise to reveal the multitasking user interface.
2. Put your finger anywhere in the multitasking user interface and move it to the right to reveal a multimedia control panel.

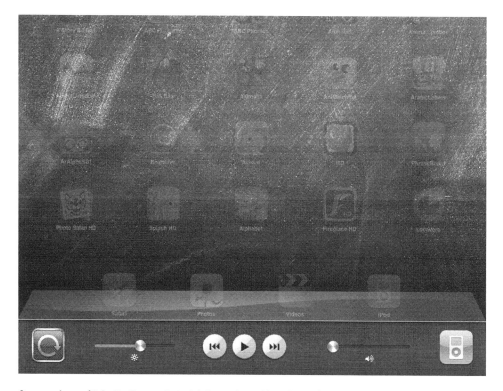

Screenshot of Media Controls in Multitasking User Interface

Using the Multitasking user interface

You will find the Multitasking user interface useful in three main ways:

1. Quickly and easily manage media controls
2. Quickly and easily switch between two or more apps
3. Troubleshoot application issues.

Quickly and Easily Switch Between Two or More Apps

Let's say you have been working with an app, you hit the home button and you launch a second app, but then you need to get back the same place you left off in the first app. For example, you are using email and then open the calendar program. You can easily return to email without having to scroll through the home screen again or using search to find the calendar.

1. In your second app, double tap the home button, and the multitasking user interface will appear

2. The app you are currently in should be the very first app icon in your list, the previous app should be the second app icon in the list
3. Tap on the icon you want to switch to, scroll to the right to see more app icons
4. Once you tap on the app icon, the iPad will open that app on your screen

Quickly and Easily Managing Media Controls

Managing media controls is an oft-needed function when using the iPad. Whether it is screen lock or volume control, it always seems to be need an adjustment. To do that in any application or directly from the home screen:

1. Double tap on the home button to launch the multitasking user interface
2. Put your finger anywhere in the multitasking user interface and move it to the right to reveal a multimedia control panel.
3. Adjust whatever setting or settings you need, for example, lock the screen rotation
4. Tap back anywhere on the main screen or single tap the home button to return to where you started

Troubleshooting Application Issues

There will be times when you want to shut down an application, for example, when it starts to act funny (i.e., it no longer produces any sound) or when you are using a Bluetooth switch interface and you want to change from one app to another. These are examples of times when shutting down and restarting just the application may be all that is needed versus shutting down the whole iPad. To shutdown a single app using the Multitasking User interface:

1. Double tap on the home button to launch the multitasking user interface.
2. Using your finger, touch and hold the app icon you want to shut down. Hold your finger there until the small red minus sign appears and the icon starts to shake, then release your finger
3. To shut down the desired app, click on the red minus sign and the app icon will disappear. This indicates that you have successfully shut down that particular app.
4. Click anywhere in the main screen or tap the home button to exit the multitasking user interface.

Controlling and Managing Access

This section is all about answering questions that are basically "How do I prevent my user from accessing this or that kind of content?" One of the primary functions of the iPad is to deliver all sorts of content to its user. This content can be in the form of video, music, images, web, text, email, etc. At its very core, the iPad is a connected device, which means you will constantly be trying to control and manage access to it. This section will cover strategies, tips and techniques to try and accomplish this goal.

Three bits of advice to keep in mind as you build your strategy:

1. When you are trying to figure out how to control content, start with the content first and work your way into the iPad and the applications that access it. This will make more sense when we get into this section
2. What you want to control now may not be what you want to control later, so as your user evolves and grows, revisit your strategy as you may want to make more content available to them
3. There are ways of controlling content without having to modify settings on the iPad; in other words, solutions to access control can be found outside of the iPad as well.

What Kinds of Content Can Be Accessed from the iPad

Let's start with defining the kinds of content that can be accessed on the iPad:

1. Images:

    -   iPad created images: Pictures taken on the camera, images that are drawn, screenshots

    -   Images from outside: Images synced via an application, like images from iPhoto® synced through iTunes into the photo application, or images from the internet saved to the photo application or in the cache.

2. Video:

    -   Video created on the iPad

    -   Video synced to the iPad video app

- Video saved from the web
- Video streaming from the web

3. Music

- Music created on the iPad
- Music synced to the iPad video app
- Music saved from the web
- Music streaming from the web

4. Web content:

- Text
- Images
- Video

5. Email - this is primarily text only, but email can also deliver

- Music
- Images
- Video

6. Application content: Applications can access data directly from the internet and either keep it on the iPad in the download data format or store the information in other iPad applications.

- Calendar/event data
- Notes with images, pictures, audio and video
- Applications can be ordered from the Apple store
- Content can be ordered within an Application as well.

Applications and Content

As you have seen from the list above, media is at the core of the iPad device, so much so that most of the technology to display and manage it is actually built into the operating system itself. As an example, that means that every application has the ability to play video. I am not saying that you will be able to watch YouTube videos in the calendar program, but you can put a YouTube link into a calendar event so that when you tap on it, the app will go to the YouTube app and play the video. Why is this important? When troubleshooting behavior, you need to understand how the content is being accessed as well as what type of content it is. Determining the content and the applications being used to access it will usually lead you to a way to manage the situation. In general, the iPad helps you manage content by its source instead of within each application. This is good for shutting down all YouTube videos, but this is bad if you just want to shut down some YouTube access.

Physically Restricting Access

In addition to electronically restricting access to the iPad, you can physically restrict access as well. You will find that other than just plain hiding the iPad from your user, you may need to:

1. Prevent them from accessing the device even if they have it in their hands
2. Prevent them from hitting the home button
3. Prevent them from touching the screen.

Prevent Them from Accessing the Device Even If They Have It in Their Hands

The simplest way to limit access to the iPad, other than hiding it, is to add a passcode to the login screen. Without entering the proper passcode, you cannot access, and therefore cannot use the iPad. Technically speaking, this is electronically restricting access, however, it's also the equivalent of locking the power button in the off position.

You can choose to make this a simple 4 digit passcode or something more complex, such as a passcode using the full keyboard. You can also choose to have the iPad erase all of the data if there are 10 unsuccessful login attempts. To activate the passcode:

1. In the **Settings** app, tap **General**, then tap **Passcode lock**
2. Tap **Turn Passcode On**, then you will enter your 4 digit passcode twice. My recommendation is that this passcode be different from the one you set for restrictions, as you may want to give them this passcode, but do not want them to be able to change the other restricted settings.
3. The **Require Passcode** setting lets you choose how long after the iPad is idle before you have to re-enter the passcode. For example, if you have it set to 5

minutes and it has been idle (i.e., in standby mode) for 4 minutes and you turn it on again, it will not ask you to re-enter the password.

4. Simple Passcode: This allows you the choice of whether or not to have a simple 4 digit passcode or a more complex one; my recommendation is to keep it simple

5. Picture Frame: If on, then the picture frame button is visible on the login screen and can be activated even if you are not logged in. If off, then the button is not visible.

6. Erase Data: My recommendation is to keep this turned off. This setting is more for data security, so if you have sensitive data on the iPad then it makes sense. Since some users may sit there and think it is fun to type in the wrong passcode, though, I would not set this to "on" as you could lose all of your data between backups.

Restricting the Home Button

When you are in a group setting - for example, if you are teaching a number of students - or even when you are one on one, there are times when you will not want to allow your user(s) to be able to activate the home button. There is no way to turn off the home button electronically, so you have to physically prevent them from tapping on the button. Your options are either to cover the button with a Bubcap, which will allow you to use many different kinds of cases, or to use a case like the iAdapter that has a built-in home screen button cover.

iAdapter
Type of Equipment: Case
Cost:
Website: www.amdi.net

The iAdapter is a case for both the iPad and iPad 2 that is specifically designed for special needs users. A key feature is a cover designed to cover the home button.

Pros:

•   Durable

•   Built for special needs

•   Home button cover.

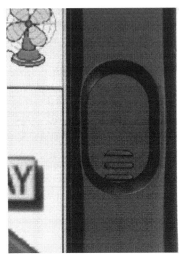

iAdapert with Closeup of Home Button Cover

Bubcap

Type of Equipment: Control Accessory
Cost: $4 per 4
Website: http://www.bubcap.com

BubCap home button covers are rigid enough to deter toddlers from pressing the home button, yet flexible enough that adults can activate the home button with a firm press. It's a similar concept to child-proof caps for medicine bottles

Pros:
- Prevents users from pressing the home screen button. By controlling the home button, you can control what the users can access.

Cons:
- Permanent. While you can remove it once you are done, it is not designed to be on some times and off others. This can prevent free-range and exploratory use of the iPad

Restricting Access to the Screen

There may be times when you may want to restrict tapping to only certain parts of the screen. Foamboard and cardboard are effective solutions to restricting access to portions of the screen. Since they are both made of paper, they will not conduct electricity, so they will not activate the screen. Plastic sheeting can also be used, but may be less cost-effective.

Electronically Restricting Access

Most of the ways you are going to be restricting access to the iPad will be through some sort of software setting. You will use:

1. **Settings** application on the iPad
2. **Settings** within an application itself.

Keep in mind that as the operating system develops, more aspects of the system will be able to be controlled as new versions are rolled out.

Restrictions Setting in the "Settings" Application

In the **Settings** application, there is a button titled **Restrictions**. This will likely be the first place you will go to manage all major content sources. By default, **Restrictions** are set to off, so you have to turn them on.

To turn on **Restrictions**:

1. Tap on the **Settings** application icon
2. Tap the **Restrictions** button
3. Tap **Enable Restrictions**
4. Enter a 4 digit passcode
5. Re-enter the 4 digit passcode

 Tip: I use a Brother P-Touch label maker and add the following information to the back of each iPad I set up:

1. Name of the iPad
2. Passcode

Depending if the back of the iPad is hidden by a case and how crafty the user is, putting the passcode on the back of the iPad may be a very bad idea.

Restrictions allows you to enable the following sources and or features:

Safari:

Safari® is the name of the default internet browser on the Apple iPad, which means that when you tap on an internet link in another application, it will automatically launch Safari. It is possible to have more than one browser installed on your iPad at a time, but it is not possible to change the default browser to anything other than Safari. This is important if you choose to turn Safari off.

When turned off, the Safari icon disappears from the home screen. Consequently, when you are in email or any other program and tap on an internet hyperlink while Safari is turned off, the hyperlink will not launch. So you can effectively shut down simple browser access to the internet.

Turning off Safari does not prevent a user from installing another browser and using that to connect to the internet, though.

Why Turn it on:

1. To be able to use Safari and access internet content from many different applications on the iPad

Why turn it off:

1. To restrict access to internet browsing through the Safari application

YouTube:

YouTube is both an application on the iPad and an internet site. Here, when you turn off YouTube, you are only turning off the YouTube application on the iPad. This is a "gotcha," so let me outline what it does and, more importantly, what it does not do:

What it does:

1. Turns off the YouTube application on the iPad. This means if you are using an app like Kideos that uses the YouTube application on the iPad to play videos,

then it will not work.

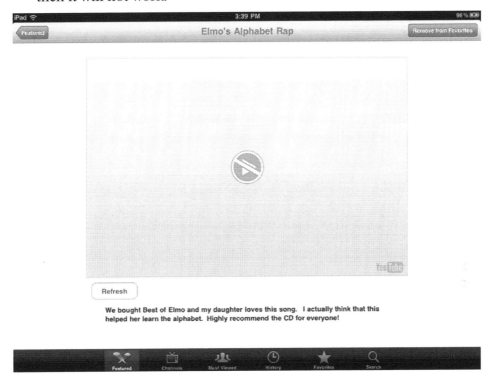

Screenshot of Kideos HD Application with YouTube Restriction Turn off

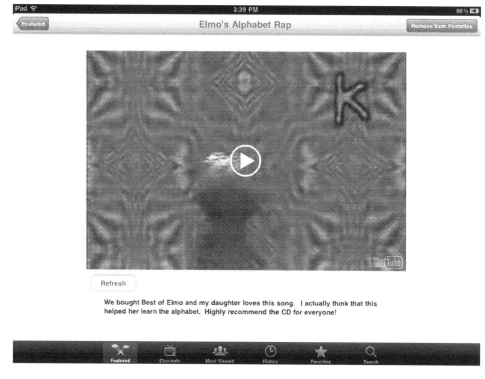

Screenshot of Kideos HD Application with YouTube Restriction Turned On

Here are some very important things that do not happen when you turn off the YouTube app:

1. You can still go to the YouTube website and play videos
2. You can go to other video websites and play videos

Why Turn it on:

1. To enable the user to watch YouTube videos in applications that use the You-Tube App

Why turn it off:

1. Prevent a user from sitting there and playing YouTube videos endlessly

Camera

The camera is a very nice feature of the iPad 2 and iPhone/iPod Touch devices. If you are using any kind of visual scheduler or symbol-to-speech program, it can be a godsend. There are times, though, when you may have a user who will sit there and take so many pictures that it can fill up the iPad's memory. Setting the Camera switch to off will disable the camera.

Why turn it on:

1. To be able to take pictures of real-world objects to incorporate into flashcards, symbol-to-speech and visual scheduling programs.

Why turn it off:

1. To prevent a user from endlessly taking pictures and filling up the iPad's memory

FaceTime

FaceTime® is a video chat or video conferencing application built into the most recent iOS devices, as well as into Apple laptop and desktop computers. It does require you to have a valid Apple ID login and access to the internet to make a connection. When you launch the program, it will grab your Apple ID from the settings, but you still have to enter your password. If the user does not know your password, then they will not able to use FaceTime. If you want to avoid the issue altogether, you can turn off FaceTime in the Settings application, and it will remove the FaceTime icon from the home screen.

Why Turn it on:

1. To allow video conferencing either between your user and their caregivers, relatives or anyone you want to allow
2. May require adult supervision

Why turn it off:

1. Will mostly be over the head of most younger users
2. May not be suitable or even valuable for some users

iTunes

Like its desktop equivalent, iTunes is an application on the iOS platform that allows you to shop for music, videos, movies, TV, podcasts, audiobooks and iTunes U content. Turning off iTunes in the restrictions tab will remove the iTunes application icon from the home screen.

Why Turn it on:

1. If you want to give your user the ability to order their own content from iTunes

Why turn it off:

1. Prevent users from ordering content (free or paid) from iTunes.

Ping

Ping is a music social network that is built into iTunes 10 and above. You can use your iPad, iPhone and iPod Touch to access the social network.

Why Turn it on:

1. If your user already uses it on their computer, this would be a natural extension of social networking

Why turn it off:

1. If you want to restrict access to social networking for your users

Installing Apps

This setting allows the user to install software directly from the App Store to the iPad. If de-selected, they can still browse apps and content in the store, but cannot install any of it. More than likely, you will want to keep this turned off. Even if you restrict what the user can install based on content age ratings, it will not prevent them from either filling up the device with a ton of free games containing ads, or, worse yet, buying a bunch of unwanted apps.

Why Turn it on: (Default)

1. Give your user the ability to download apps and content on their own

Why turn it off: (recommended for most special needs users)

1. Restrict your users from installing software from the App Store.

Deleting Apps

This feature allows you to turn off the ability to delete apps from the iPad. Deleting an app from the iPad does not change the fact that you have purchased the app, nor does it permanently remove it from your iTunes backup. Deleting the app simply means removing it from that iPad's home screen.

Why Turn it on: (Default)

1. If you want your users to be able to remove apps from the Home screen.

Why turn it off: (recommended for most special needs users)

1. Most of the time, you will want to turn this setting off, mainly because it is very easy to unintentionally remove apps from the home screen. I have seen apps wiped from the home screen one by one by kids because they think it is fun. To prevent that, and possibly disorientation, my recommendation is to prevent end users from being able to delete apps

Location

The location services refers to the iPad's built-in GPS receiver. There are apps, like the Map app, that use the location service to display information, or it can be used for any number of other reasons. There are three major ways you can use the Location Setting. The first is to decide whether to keep the service turned on (default) or to turn it off. Then you need to decide which programs will have access to the GPS service. For example, does your drum program really need the location service turned on? Lastly, you need to decide how you are going to handle new programs. If you select allow changes to the settings, this will allow new programs to automatically gain access to the location service. Selecting "do not allow changes" means any new applications installed will not have access to the location service.

The default setting is to allow access to every program that requests it. I think for the most part, most special needs users do not really need GPS, with the possible exception of adults. If you think about it, GPS is mostly used for navigation, or to relay information to you, such as a program that uses GPS to know where you are to be able to suggest food that is in season, for example. While this is beneficial information and, in the above cases, information that just stays on the iPad itself, there are ways this information can be transmitted to other systems. For example, using some social network platforms, you can take a picture of some location or post a status, and using the GPS it will post up the location where the status was entered or where the picture was taken for anyone to see. So, theoretically, anyone who has access to the post knows where the person making the post was at that moment in time. For a younger child, this would make me very uncomfortable.

Why Turn it on: (Default)

1. If you regularly use apps that rely upon the GPS feature
2. If your users are mature enough to make their own decisions

Why turn it off: (recommended)

1. Even if you keep the feature turned on, consider turning off any app that you know does not need it. (recommended)
2. Consider turning on the "Don't Allow" feature to prevent new apps from automatically being able to use the GPS feature
3. Be aware of which apps do try to use it, and try to determine why; if you don't know or if they don't make sense (why a visual drum needs GPS, for example) then turn them off.

Accounts

Accounts has two options: **Allow Changes** and **Don't Allow Changes**. If you keep the default setting and allow changes, then anyone can change the Apple ID under the Store Tab in settings. This an important feature to understand for a number of reasons:

1. If you use the iPad to download content using another account, you would not know that the iPad had an unauthorized app until you backed it up using iTunes. Then you would get an app authorization warning stating the new app is not registered to that particular iTunes account.
2. The good news is that just switching the Apple ID does not change the restric-

tions setting on the iPad itself, so the user would still be limited to whatever content you allowed them to view.

Why Turn it on: (Default is to allow changes)

1. If you want to switch Apple ID accounts on your iPad.

Why turn it off: (Recommended)

1. I recommend turning this off to prevent a user from switching accounts, downloading content and then switching back.

In-App Purchases

In-App Purchases allows you to buy upgrade packs for applications while still in the app instead of having to exit and launch the App Store. Some apps are designed as a lite version that can be upgraded to a full version; some in-app purchases extend the full app even further. You have the ability to turn In-App Purchases on or off globally, but not individually. The important point to note is that even if In-App Purchases is turned on and a user tries to make a purchase, they still need to know the password of the Apple ID to execute the transaction and install the app. So this really only becomes an issue if they know the Apple ID password.

Why Turn it on: (Default)

1. If you want to be able to make in-app purchases

Why turn it off: (Recommended)

1. If you want to prevent in-app purchasing buttons and pop-ups from showing up every time some apps are launched. In general, I like to reduce the amount of ads my users see and not distract them with unnecessary decisions. Particularly since I don't allow them to make their own purchases, I feel like a pop-up or button telling them to buy something they cannot is unnecessary.

Ratings For

This setting selects what country's ratings system you want to use to restrict downloaded content or applications. For example, if you select the United States and you look at the movie rating systems, you will see G, PG, PG-13, R, NC-17; select

Australia and they will change to G, PG, M, MA15+, R18. You should select the rating system you best understand and with which you are most comfortable.

Music and Podcasts

The only setting under **Music & Podcasts** is the ability to allow or exclude explicit content. This only works if the content comes through the App Store. Content that comes through other sources, such as a MP3 music downloaded from the internet and synced via iTunes may have explicit content, but may not be flagged "Explicit" and would therefore not be edited by this filter.

 Recommendation: Do not allow explicit content AND make sure to monitor all content that is used on this device.

Movies

This group of settings gives you the ability to set the content level of movies that are displayed on the iPad in the Video application or the App Store. For example, if you buy a rated R movie on your iTunes equipped pc and it is set to automatically download all movies to your iPad, if your iPad is set to restrict any movie rated above PG-13, you would not see that movie in the list of movies in the Video program. If you were to change your settings, you would then see the movie in the list.

An important note, this only applies to commercial videos bought through the App Store or iTunes. Home movies or DVDs converted to video files, uploaded to iTunes and synced to the iPad do not have any ratings built-in, so they would all be considered G. Unless all of your content is sourced from Apple, do not assume that the content can be controlled through this setting.

 Recommendation: If you control all of the content that is added to the device then you will automatically be picking appropriate content; if you allow the users to buy and/or download their own content, then set this to a level that is appropriate for your users.

TV Shows

This group of settings gives you the ability to set the content level of TV Shows that are displayed on the iPad in the Video application or App Store. For example, if you were to have this set to TV-G, then you would not see any content over TV-G in either playback applications such as the Video app or available for order or download from the App Store.

Important note, this also only applies to commercially sourced TV programs and would not apply to any homemade video. That said, all homemade videos or otherwise sourced material is classified as Video, so any settings involving TV Shows would not apply.

 Recommendation: If you control all of the content that is added to the device then you will automatically be picking appropriate content; if you allow the users to buy and/or download their own content, then set this to a level that is appropriate for your users.

Apps

This group of settings gives you the ability to set the content level of the Applications that are displayed and therefore available for selection and download in the App Store. "4+" means it is suitable for children ages 4 and up. During the submission process to Apple, each app in the App Store gets an age rating assigned to it. The idea is that the age rating listed will help you to select the right apps for your user. Generally speaking, this is a good system. However, you will find that some apps, particularly games, may have content or themes in them that are more appropriate for older children than the rating assigned indicates.

 Recommendation: If you control all of the content that is added to the device then you will automatically be picking appropriate content; if you allow your users to buy and/or download their own content, then set this to a level that is appropriate for your users.

Game Center

Game Center is an application across all of Apple's mobile devices that allows you connect and play games with other people. In some cases, these are people you know; in other cases, it may be people you don't know. You will have to log into the game center application on the iPad with an Apple ID. From there, you can make a friend request to other people and keep a friend list. In order to have your own Apple ID, you need to be 13 or older, and if you are below age 18, you also need parental permission. Game Center already assumes you are 13 or older.

There is no way to turn off Game Center or remove it from the Home Screen, so if you want to completely prevent its use, do not give the user an Apple ID. Bear in mind they could create one by themselves if they are savvy. If you decide you want to allow them to access and use Game Center, you still have two important ways of controlling access.

You have two options under Game Center to control access:

1. Allow Multiplayer Games: Keep this on (Default) if you have older users who do a lot of gaming and like to game with their siblings or friends. This only works if the game has the feature and you have two devices that both have the same game. Turn it off you want to control that feature or if you don't want them to able to use it.
2. Adding Friends: You will likely want to turn this off. (Recommended and not default). Turning this off prevents the user from being able to make friend requests and connect with anyone new. As a strategy, you can set up a group of friends for your user and then turn the **Adding Friends** feature off to prevent them from adding anyone else or, more importantly, anyone unknown to you.

Internet

There are may aspects to controlling internet access on the iPad. The iPad by its very definition is an internet device. Many aspects of how it works are designed to connect to the internet. A major concern with the iPad is the ability of the user to access content on the internet that you find to be inappropriate for that user. In this section, we are going to focus on the following topics:

1. No browser access
2. Some browser Access and Safari Settings
3. Restricting access through the network rather than at the device level

No Browser Access

There will be times when you do not want your user to have access to the internet. In other words, you want to prevent them from browsing. There are three main tasks you have to perform to prevent them from using the iPad to browse the internet.

1. Enable Restrictions: Go to **Settings**, then the **General** tab, then **Restrictions** and **Enable Restriction**. You will have to create a 4 digit passcode and type it in twice; please remember this passcode and do not let your user know the number.

2. Turn off Safari. To do this go to **Settings**, the **General** tab, **Restrictions** and **Enable Restrictions**, then turn off Safari.

3. Prevent Adding Apps: To do this go to **Settings**, **General** tab, **Restrictions** and turn off **Installing Apps**.

Combining these two settings will prevent the user from using Safari, the default browser, to access the internet and also prevent them from being able to install a new browser.

Some Browser Access and Safari Settings

Rather than preventing any internet access, you may want to allow either some internet or all internet access. The biggest issue that arises is that, unlike movies or TV shows, there is no universal ratings system for the internet. The lack of a ratings system also means there is no way to restrict content using the default browser. Before we get into alternate ways of restricting content, though, I do want to cover Safari settings to make sure you know that they are.

Safari Settings

In the Settings app under the Safari tab here are the settings you will find:

1. Search Engine: The default is Google; I would select the search engine with which you are the most comfortable from the available list.

2. AutoFill: By default, this is turned off. There are two aspects to AutoFill you can turn on

- Use Contact Info: When turned on, select your contact record from the list of contacts and every time you need to fill out a form with your contact information, Safari will use the information stored in the record you selected to do so. Make sure your contact record is complete and accurate.

- Names and passwords: If turned on, it will store your user name and password the first time you type them in Safari and then retrieve them as needed the next time you go to that site and login. There is also the ability to clear the list as well.

- Recommendation: I leave AutoFill turned off. I don't like portable devices to have user names and passwords stored in them. With good data management habits, though, this can be a safe way to store information. But the important thing is that you have to have good data management habits.

Restricting Internet Access Using Other Browsers

An alternative to using Safari to browse the internet is to select a specialty browser. There are many different specialty browsers on the market. When it comes to restricting content, there are two main ways to accomplish this.

1. Monitor content: Monitor content is just that, using different technology, you can monitor words, images and video. This can be done manually or electronically or using a combination of both, thereby determining the appropriateness of the content. This is usually based upon age or academic level, such as elementary school level. The advantage of this strategy is that as the internet grows, this can expand automatically with it.

2. Monitoring Address: Monitoring Address is done based on internet domain name or address. So for example if you restrict YouTube, then any time you type YouTube.com in the browser, it will deny access. The advantage of this strategy is that you can create a very restricted and controlled environment for your user.

 Mobicip Safe Browser

Cost: $5
Developer: Mobicip.com
iTunes URL: *http://itunes.apple.com/us/app/mobicip-safe-browser/id299153586?mt=8*

The Mobicip Safe Browser filters content based on an age range you select. You can select among Elementary, Middle or High school as an age range. There are three ways it protects your user:

1. The browser monitors searches by the user,
2. All content is analyzed using its own technology for inappropriate content
3. The company has built its own database categorizing and cataloging new websites as they are created.

The advantage of this application is that you can set your level once and the software manages the content. Your user is then free to roam and explore. This strategy of free exploration may be better suited for older and more mature users. The disadvantage of it is that you could still be allowing them access to content you may not want them to be consuming.

 Recommendation: Use this app for more mature users who are ready to explore the internet independently and use this app as training wheels.

Screenshot of Mobicip Safe Browser

 ## Safe Web for kids
Cost: $2
Developer: Bobgoo
iTunes URL: *http://itunes.apple.com/us/app/safe-web-for-kids/id460723131?mt=8*

Safe Web for Kids allows you to restrict access to website domains that you select.

You build a list of domains that your user is permitted to access; they cannot access anything else. The advantage here is that it is very controlled and restricted. The disadvantage is twofold:

1. Because it is domain-based in how it restricts, you would have to restrict all of YouTube when you may only want to restrict some content on YouTube.
2. You will spend some time developing an appropriate list of domains.

 Recommendation: This app is great for young and or less mature users, where you would want to have complete control of their internet experience.

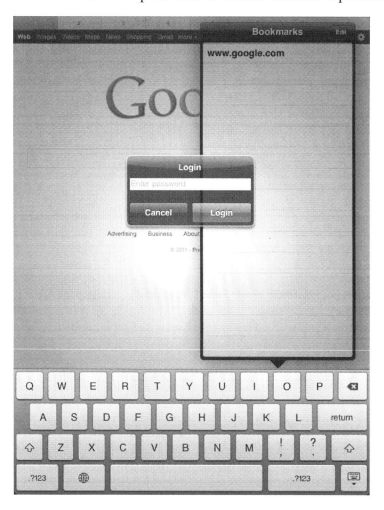

Screenshot of Safe Web for kids

Restricting Access Through the Network, Not at the Device Level

You can also control access to the internet at the network level rather than at the device level. The advantage of monitoring and restricting at the network level is that no matter what device or browser is used, the restrictions are enforced. The disadvantage is that even if the highest level of restriction is not appropriate or desired by everyone using the network, it is enforced across the network. Here are some options:

1. Filtering from ISP (internet services provider). Most major internet service providers have some sort of parental control system in place. See your ISP for more details
2. Filtering at the Router. The router is a device that connects your network to the internet. There are routers that offer filtering services and/or software that allows you to set parental controls. See your router manufacturer's website for additional information.
3. Monitoring Software: There is software that will monitor internet usage and may or may not be designed to block certain types of traffic. Search for "accountability software" or "internet monitoring software" in your favorite browser.

CHAPTER

Accessibility Features

Apple has a long history of including accessibility features into their core design. The iPad is no exception. In this chapter, I will highlight these core features, explain how they work and how they might be used. Like everything to do with assistive technology and accessibility, it is all about the needs of the end user. Those needs determine what is a usable feature and what is not. Experimentation will be needed as you and your user work through how you are going to use this technology to get the most from it.

I will start you off with this thought. One of the instructors in my assistive technology class was talking about his iPad and how it is one of the best devices he has to "read" his email. He loves it. He could not live without the device. The instructor has been blind his whole life and was using a built in technology called VoiceOver to have the iPad read his email back to him. And while he cannot see the screen, he uses it constantly.

Apple Accessibility Resources

Apple has a number of resources for special needs, assistive technology and accessibility. An internet search will provide the latest information, but here are a number of links that I have found to be helpful:

Apple

1. Apple Accessibility page: *http://www.apple.com/accessibility/*
2. Apple Accessibility Resources page: *http://www.apple.com/accessibility/resources/*
3. Apple iOS 5 HTML Manual (US english): *http://manuals.info.apple.com/en_US/ipad_user_guide.pdf*
4. Apple iOS 5 PDF Manual (US english): *http://www.apple.com/accessibility/resources/*
5. Apple Accessibility for Developers (for iOS): *http://developer.apple.com/library/ios/#documentation/UserExperience/Conceptual/iPhoneAccessibility/Introduction/Introduction.html*
6. Braille Displays from Apple: *http://www.apple.com/accessibility/voiceover/devicesupport.html*

Apple Accessibility Features

Apple has spent a lot of time building accessibility features into both its mobile operating system and into the hardware design. When you talk to Apple folks, they often say - and rightfully so - that Apple has accessibility built into its DNA. Apple organizes its accessibility features by impairment:

1. Vision
2. Hearing
3. Physical and Motor Skill

In the practical world of assistive technology implementation, impairment is less effective than looking at skill building. That said, you need to start somewhere, and for continuity and because someone may open this book and want to see one of these broad categories, in this chapter I will keep the features under the same broad categories that Apple does. Keep this in mind: a feature you can use is a feature you can use. Period. Further, if you can adapt another feature designed for something else, you should. Experiment and find things that work, both high and low tech.

Apple Vision Accessibility list

Under the Vision category, Apple includes the following features:

1. VoiceOver - Screen reading technology
2. Zoom - Ability to control screen zoom independent of the application
3. White on Black - the ability to reverse the foreground and background text colors
4. Speak Auto Text -
5. Speak Selection - the ability to highlight a section of text and have it spoken it back to you.
6. Tactile Buttons - Design feature where the primary buttons are physical buttons not touch sensitive screen buttons
7. Headset Compatibility -
8. Audible Alerts

VoiceOver Introduction

VoiceOver is a screen reader built into the iPad. It will read the text on the screen from the upper left corner (in English) to the lower right corner. As it reads each item, it also selects that item. Double tap while an item is selected and it will launch that item or do whatever a single tap would do if VoiceOver was turned off. Using gestures, you can control how the program works; for example, a single flick right will go to the next item. VoiceOver was designed to not only help people with limited to no vision be able to use the iPad effectively, but also to help those with reading and reading comprehension issues as well. There are a number of settings that can be customized using VoiceOver.

VoiceOver will accommodate different languages. For example, VoiceOver can be used to read back an Arabic typing program. In a test of the system, VoiceOver read each of the letters to me properly on the keyboard, but was unable to read the words correctly. For some Arabic programs, it was not able to read any Arabic letters back to me at all. This suggests that the programmer must also take VoiceOver into account when the app is created. As a consequence, there may be some applications that just do not perform well with VoiceOver simply because they were not designed with this feature in mind. Like many things for those with special needs, you will have to experiment to see what works and what does not.

While I have witnessed how effective VoiceOver can be for those with visual impairments, I would not consider myself a pro on this issue. So while I will discuss how to set it up, and any tips or tricks I have learned along the way, if you and your target user are serious about implementing the iPad and you have a visual impairment, you should consult with your therapists and together develop a plan for the most effective use of this feature.

VoiceOver Activiaton and Setup

VoiceOver Settings can be found under Settings/General/Accessibility.

1. To activate VoiceOver, tap on the VoiceOver off tab to turn it on.
2. This will then unhide the VoiceOver Practice Button
3. **Speak Hints**: the default is on. If Speak Hints are turned on, VoiceOver will communicate any available actions that can be taken when it scrolls over a particular area of the screen. It will also, if available, provide any instructions that the program includes for use with VoiceOver.
4. **Speaking Rate**: Speed Slider: This is a slider that can be used to increase (Rabbit) or decrease (Turtle) the speed of the voice used for VoiceOver
5. **Typing Feedback**:

    •   Software Keyboard: You can select Characters and Words, just words, just characters, or nothing as feedback

    •   Hardware Keyboard: You can select to have Characters and Words, just words, just characters, or nothing as feedback

6. Use **Phonetics**: (Default is On) If selected, VoiceOver will read the character and then attempt its phonetic equivalent.
7. Use **Pitch Change**: (Default is On), VoiceOver will use a higher pitch when speaking the first item in a list or other type of group. When active, this will also apply to the first letter of a group of letters. VoiceOver will also use a lower pitch at the end of a group of words or letters to indicate an end.
8. Use **Compact Voice**: (Default is Off) When selected, the VoiceOver voice is truncated and more dense sounding. As you get used to VoiceOver, compacting the voice is a way of getting a little more efficiency from the experience.
9. **Braille**: This setting allows you to control the braille settings on the iPad. The iPad supports a number of Bluetooth braille displays

    •   Contracted Braille: (Default is Off)

- Eight-Dot Braille: (Default is On)

- Status Cell: (Default is OFF) other options are Left or Right

10. **Rotor**: The Rotor setting allows you to select the items you want to have in your VoiceOver Rotor. Simply tap to turn on or off the item to add or remove it from the rotor. You can tap, hold and drag (on the 3 lines icon in each row) to change the order of the items on the list.

11. **Language Rotor**: Allows you to select the languages you want to have in your language rotor. You can tap, hold and drag (on the 3 lines icon in each row) to change the order of the items on the list.

12. **Navigate Images**: Allows you to choose to keep all images, identify no images or only images with a description

- Always (Default)

- With description

- Never

13. **Speak Notification**: (Default is Off) When off, VoiceOver will only speak the time when unlocking the iPad.

VoiceOver Practice Area

When you select this button, you will find yourself in an area where you can practice the various VoiceOver gestures. As you make each gesture, it will speak the gesture, and what each gesture will do - for example "single flick to the right" and "advance to next item."

Screenshot of VoiceOver Practice Area

VoiceOver Gestures

Gestures to navigate and read

- **Tap:** Speak item.
- **Flick right or left:** Select the next or previous item.
- **Flick up or down:** Depends on the Rotor Control setting.
- **Two-finger tap:** Stop speaking the current item.
- **Two-finger flick up:** Read all from the top of the screen.
- **Two-finger flick down:** Read all from the current position.

- **Two-finger "scrub":** Move two fingers back and forth three times quickly (making a "z") to dismiss an alert or go back to the previous screen.

- **Two-finger triple tap:** Open the Item Chooser.

- **Three-finger flick up or down:** Scroll one page at a time.

- **Three-finger flick right or left:** Go to the next or previous page (such as the Home screen, Stocks, or Safari).

- **Three-finger tap:** Speak additional information, such as position within a list or whether text is selected.

- **Four-finger tap at top of screen:** Select the first item on the page.

- **Four-finger tap at bottom of screen:** Select the last item on the page.

While an item is Active

- **Double-tap:** Activate the selected item.

- **Triple-tap:** Double-tap an item.

- **Split-tap:** An alternative to selecting an item and double-tapping is to touch an item with one finger, then tap the screen with another to activate an item.

- **Touch an item with one finger, tap the screen with another finger** ("split-tapping"): Activate the item.

- **Double-tap and hold (1 second) + standard gesture:** Use a standard gesture. The double-tap and hold gesture tells the iPad to interpret the subsequent gesture as standard. For example, you can double-tap and hold, then without lifting your finger, drag your finger to slide a switch.

- **Two-finger double-tap:** Play or pause in Music, Videos, YouTube, Voice Memos, or Photos. Take a photo with the camera. Start or pause recording in Camera or Voice Memos. Start or stop the stopwatch.

- **Two-finger double-tap and hold:** Open the element labeler.

- **Two-finger triple-tap:** Open the Item Chooser.

- **Three-finger double-tap:** Mute or un-mute VoiceOver.

- **Three-finger triple-tap:** Turn the screen curtain on or off

An important note about VoiceOver and Gestures, when VoiceOver is turned on, VoiceOver gestures control the iPad, not the standard gestures.

Tip: You can use VoiceOver to read stories and PDF documents. So if you have issues with reading comprehension, or simply would like the iPad to read to you, VoiceOver can be used for this purpose. Note, if you want VoiceOver to read PDF files, then the PDF files need to be text-based and not scans of documents.

Tip: Under Settings/General/Accessibility/Triple-click Home to VoiceOver on the iPad. Once set, you can turn on or off VoiceOver by triple-tapping the home button. This is particularly useful for group settings where the iPad will be used with and without VoiceOver.

Zoom

Zoom is an accessibility feature of the iPad that allows you enlarge a portion of the screen and magnify its contents independent of any features built into the application. It is application independent as well, so it works with all apps, either Apple's or those by a third party developer. It can be used within an app, on the home screen or anywhere on the iPad.

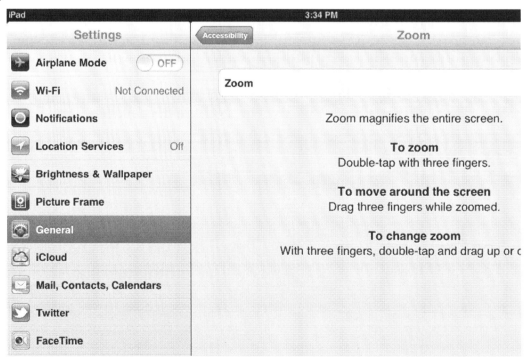

Screenshot of Screen Zoomed in 135%

Zoom Activation

To turn on Zoom:

1. Within **Settings, General, Accessibility,** select **Zoom,**
2. Select **On**

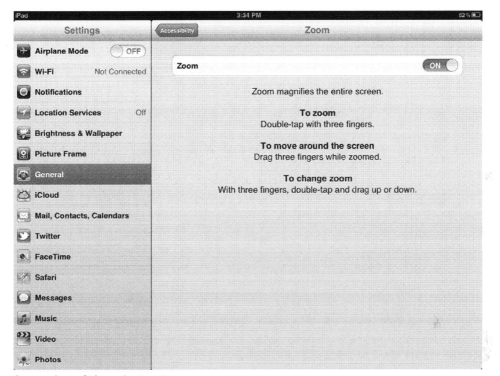

Screenshot of Zoom Activation

How to Use Zoom

Once Zoom is activated, it is controlled by using a three fingered set of gestures:

To Zoom: Using 3 fingers, double tap the screen to zoom in on the location of the tap

To scroll around once in Zoom mode: Tap and drag with 3 fingers in the opposite direction you want to scroll. For example, if you are viewing the lower left hand corner of the screen and want to view the upper left hand corner, tap with 3 fingers anywhere on the screen, then drag your finger down. This will scroll the screen upwards.

To Increase or decrease Zoom: Double Tap with 3 fingers, then drag up to increase zoom factor; double tap with 3 fingers and drag down to decrease zoom. Zoom factor will be remembered when you turn zoom on or off. In fact, it is remembered even if you turn off the zoom setting altogether in the settings and later turn it back on.

White on Black

White on black is a way of reversing the foreground and background color for all content on the screen. It works independently of the application and is designed to help people who need a different level of contrast when reading text. Here is the same screenshot with and without White on Black turned on.

iPad 📶   3:03 PM   Not Charging 🔋

People With Multiple Chemical Sensitivity (MCS) and Respiratory Disabilities

PEOPLE WITH MCS AND RESPIRATORY DISABILITIES such as asthma or emphysema react to toxins in the air. Stale air, fumes from cleaning products, perfume, carpeting, air freshener or even the fumes from magic markers can trigger a severe reaction.

◆ Try to avoid spray-cleaning tables, windows or other surfaces while people are in your place of business. If you must use a spray product, spray or pour it closely into the cloth, not into the air. Use less-toxic products when possible. Request that staff that have contact with the public go easy on fragranced body-care products like cologne, hair spray, hand lotion, and after-shave.

◆ Maintaining good ventilation and indoor air quality will not only benefit your customers who have MCS and respiratory disabilities, it will also help you and all of your employees stay healthier and more alert.

Screenshot of Text with White on Black Turned Off. This the Default Setting

iPad 🛜   3:03 PM   Not Charging 🔋

People With Multiple Chemical Sensitivity (MCS) and Respiratory Disabilities

PEOPLE WITH MCS AND RESPIRATORY DISABILITIES such as asthma or emphysema react to toxins in the air. Stale air, fumes from cleaning products, perfume, carpeting, air freshener or even the fumes from magic markers can trigger a severe reaction.

◆ Try to avoid spray-cleaning tables, windows or other surfaces while people are in your place of business. If you must use a spray product, spray or pour it closely into the cloth, not into the air. Use less-toxic products when possible. Request that staff that have contact with the public go easy on fragranced body-care products like cologne, hair spray, hand lotion, and after-shave.

◆ Maintaining good ventilation and indoor air quality will not only benefit your customers who have MCS and respiratory disabilities, it will also help you and all of your employees stay healthier and more alert.

Screenshot of Text with White on Black Turned On.

How to Activate White on Black

To activate White on Black:

1. Go to **Settings**, **General, Accessibility**, **White on Black**. The Default is off.
2. Tap slider to turn **On**.

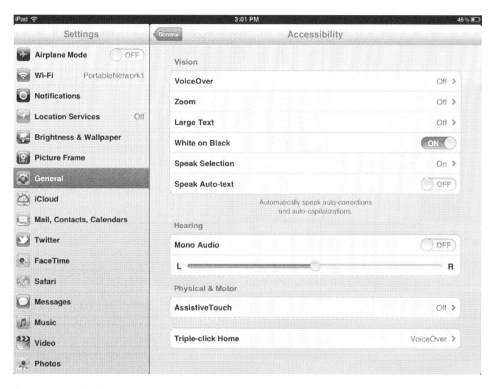

Screenshot of White on Black Activation Toggle

Large Text

Apple has built in the ability to choose a larger text size for your default text. You have 6 choices, from 20 point to 56 point text. This does not change every text on the iPad. The application has to be built to take advantage of this feature. For example, a PDF in iBook did not change text size (I would not expect it to) but email in the Mail program did (which I did expect to have happen). You will mainly find this feature available in text related applications. Unfortunately, it is unlikely to appear in most application menu items, so I would not count on this feature for navigation, but more for reading. Use zoom instead.

Screenshot of email with Large Text Turned Off

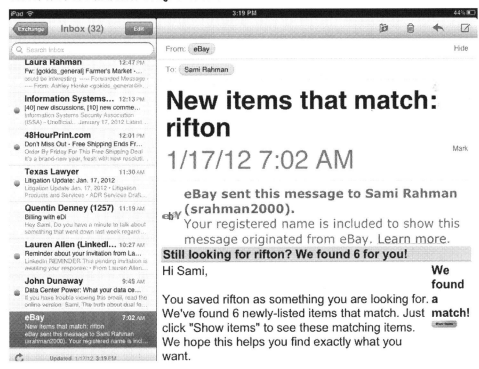

Screenshot of email with Large Text Turned On

How to Activate Large Text

How to turn Large Text on:

1. Go to **Settings**, **General, Accessibility**, and tap on **Large Text**. The Default is off.
2. Select the size of type you would like from the list.

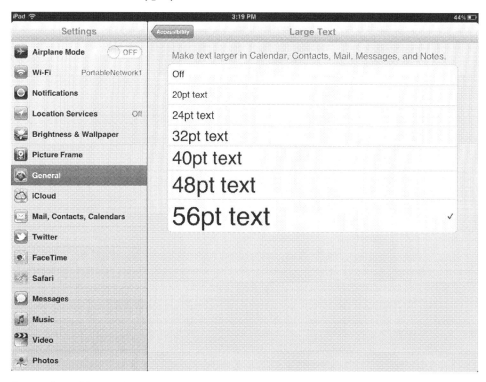

Screenshot of Large Text Type Size Selection

Speak Selection

Speak selection is a feature that can be activated, and will allow the iPad to read a selection of text back to you. The default setting for this feature is off, but once activated, it adds a Speak button to your highlight text menu. When this button is pushed, it reads back any text that is highlighted. It only works with applications that are VoiceOver enabled and in the current VoiceOver languages. I use it when I come across words that are new to me and I may not recognize and to read back sentences that for whatever reason don't make sense to me when I read them.

Screenshot of Speak Button in Action

How to Activate Speak Selection

Speak Selection will speak any selected text you highlight. To activate the feature:

1. Go to **Settings**, **General**, **Accessibility**, tap **Speak Selection**
2. Turn on to activate
3. Adjust Speaking rate using the Speaking rate slider

Tactile Buttons

The iPad's main buttons are tactile physical buttons. This is important as an accessibility feature in that a lot of technology employs surface touch or "soft" buttons. Soft buttons can be very difficult to use if you do not have good eyesight or fine motor control. While applications on the iPad utilize all sorts of "soft buttons," the fact that the main controls are all tactile physical buttons makes the iPad shine as an accessible device.

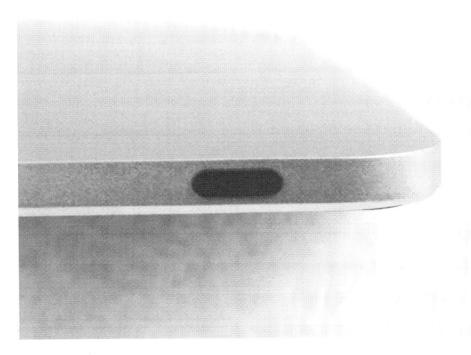

Photo iPad 1 Power Button

Headset Compatibility

While a headset is considered standard on most consumer electronics designed to deliver media, the iPad headset jack has the ability be used as a microphone jack as well. This kind of multipurpose jack is often used with cell phones to incorporate a wired headset and microphone combination. Both listening to the audio via head phones, wired or not, and the ability to plug in a microphone and use applications that allow you to record your voice can be of great advantage in many special need circumstances.

Audible Alerts

There are a number of audible alerts that can be set on the iPad:

1. Text Tone
2. New Mail
3. Sent Mail
4. Tweet
5. Calendar Alerts
6. Reminder Alerts

7. Keyboard Clicks

In most cases you can choose what ringtone or alerts you want for each item.

How to Activate Audible Alerts

There are a number of audible alerts that can be adjusted to suit your needs and tastes:

1. Go to **Settings**, **General**, and tap on **Sounds**
2. Under Sounds you will see a long list of alerts you can adjust
3. Tap on the one you want
4. Select from the list of available tones or ringtones or click to buy more.

Tones are short sounds; ringtones are longer more elaborate sounds. I would recommend short and sweet over hearing a whole opera every time you get an email. That said, to each his or her own. Opera away if that is your thing.

Apple Hearing Impaired List

Under the Hearing category, Apple includes the following features:

1. FaceTime
2. Closed Captioning
3. Headphone Jack
4. Bluetooth Audio
5. Mono Audio
6. Messages with iMessage
7. Visual Alerts

FaceTime

FaceTime is video conferencing software that can be used between two different Apple products. You can use FaceTime with any combination of iPad, iPod Touch, iPhone, Mac Desktop or laptop. Video conference can be used as a way to read lips or be used with video or text relay services. Video relay services use a translator to translate speech into either sign language or into text and vice versa. Video and text relay services allow those with hearing impairments to be able to communicate freely. FaceTime and video conferencing can also be used to promote social interaction.

To use FaceTime, you must sign up using your name and a valid email address. You can find other FaceTime users via a search based on first name, last name and/or email address. You then add users to your contacts. If you have a lot of contacts, you may want to use the favorites list to readily access those contacts you most frequently use. Tap on a contact and it will call them. If they are available and willing, they will answer. Then a video conference session starts and away you go.

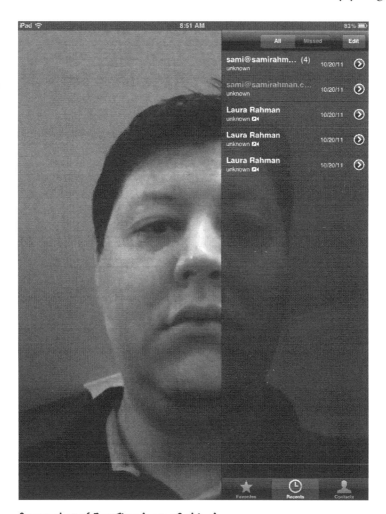

Screenshot of FaceTime (note: 2 chins)

Tip: We use FaceTime with Noah and his grandparents who live out of state. He interacts better with a video than just over the phone. It forces him come out of his shell more and allows him to see his grandparents smile and interact with him. It also helps his grandparents see him grow and develop. They do it about once a week.

Relay Services That Can Be Used with FaceTime

Video relay services use a translator to translate speech into either sign language or into text and vice versa. Here is a list of video relay services that can be used with FaceTime:

1. Communication Services For the Deaf, Inc: *www.zvrs.com* You call them on the phone and then start a FaceTime chat.
2. IWRelay (subcontractor of Healinc Telecom, LLC.): *www.iwrelay.com*. They have an app you use to dial your number. When an interpreter comes online, you are able to then trigger a FaceTime chat.
3. Purple Communication Inc.: *www.purple.us/iphone* Purple does not use FaceTime but uses their own video conference software.

Not all services are free to the hearing impaired, so please check with the provider you want to use to understand any fees that may apply.

How to Setup FaceTime for the First Time

To set up and activate FaceTime for the first time you will need to do two things, turn FaceTime on and set up your FaceTime account:

1. Go to **Settings**, **FaceTime** and tap on the **ON/Off** Slider to turn on

2. Go to **Settings**, **FaceTime,** tap **create new account.** (This can also be done inside the FaceTime app as well)

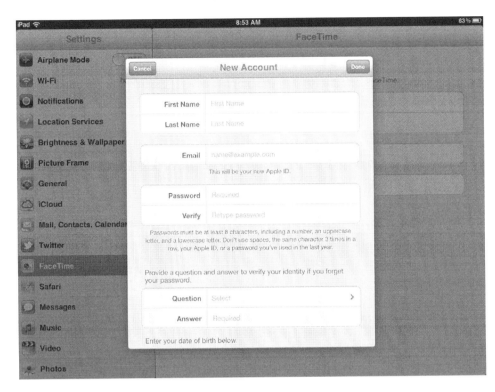

Screenshot of FaceTime create new account form

To create a FaceTime account, provide the following information:

1. First Name
2. Last Name
3. Valid Email Address
4. Password
5. Security Question of your choosing
6. Security Answer

 Notes:

1. Your FaceTime account does not need to be your Apple ID, though it can be,
2. Your account can be the same account you use for other Apple services such as iMessage
3. You do need to have access to the email address you use, as Apple will send you a confirmation email that you must validate before you can use FaceTime
4. First Name, Last Name and email address are searchable by anyone on Face-Time. It is public information, so I do not allow my kids to have their own

accounts. Only my wife and I do, and when we want to use it with my kids, we just use our accounts with their grandparents.

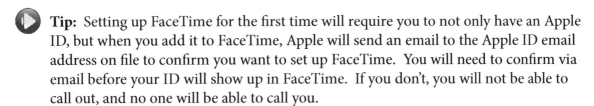

Tip: Setting up FaceTime for the first time will require you to not only have an Apple ID, but when you add it to FaceTime, Apple will send an email to the Apple ID email address on file to confirm you want to set up FaceTime. You will need to confirm via email before your ID will show up in FaceTime. If you don't, you will not be able to call out, and no one will be able to call you.

Tip: FaceTime relies on an internet connection for both devices. Use the strongest internet connection you have available. If you are using an iPad, iPod Touch, or iPhone, be as close to your wi-fi receiver as you can. This will ensure you have the strongest signal. If you are using a Mac desktop or laptop, use a wired ethernet connection. Only use a high speed internet connection. Theoretically, your internet connection will be slower than both ethernet and wifi connections. It may or may not be slower than your 3G connection.

Type of Internet connection Strongest to Weakest	Devices	Notes
Ethernet Cable	Mac Desktop or Laptop	
Wi-fi	Mac Desktop or Laptop, iPad, iPod Touch, iPhone	Fastest if close to Wi-Fi Receiver/Transmitter
3G	iPad, iPod Touch, iPhone (Mac Desktop or Laptop if you have a 3G card)	Quality will depend on signal from tower. Sometimes great other times will not work.

Tip: If you have a communal iPad or other device on which you will use FaceTime, and you have a number of users who are old enough and mature enough to need their own contact lists, you can set up multiple FaceTime accounts. This way, a user can login as themselves and only see what they need to see. I am mainly talking about contacts, call history and favorites. For example, when I set up the FaceTime account for my mother-in-law, it only has two contacts - her daughters - since that is all she needs. She gets on FaceTime and goes to favorites (or contacts since she only has two) and sees exactly who she needs to see.

Note: Keep in mind that First Name, Last Name and Email address are all publicly searchable.

Closed Captioning

The iPad video player supports media that has closed captioning text embedded within it. This can be from a commercial source such as iTunes. You can also create your own video and add closed captioning. As long as the closed captioning is in the standard closed captioning format within the video, it will play and display properly in the Video application.

How to Activate Closed Captioning

To activate closed captioning on Apple's video player:

5. Go to **Settings**, **Video**, tap the **Closed Captioning On/Off** slider from the default off to on.

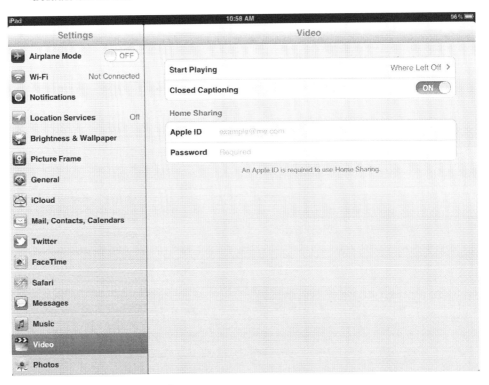

Screenshot of Settings, Video Settings

 Note: This setting only applies to the Video application. Other applications have to have their own ability to display closed captioning

Headphone Jack

iPads have a 3.4 millimeter headphone jack. This can be used by both headphones and speakers. The speakers and headphones can either be amplified or not. The headphone jack can also support a microphone/headphone combination such as that often used with cellphones. The point being that it is not only an output jack but also an input jack.

Bluetooth Audio

The iPad has support for Bluetooth audio devices. This means you can connect a wireless headphone or speaker. Both of these devices can have amplification for those with hearing impairments. Note that any Bluetooth device will require its own power source, so with Bluetooth accessories, take into account battery life and charging.

How to Activate Bluetooth

Connecting a Bluetooth audio device to an iPad is a two step process.

Step 1: Turn on Bluetooth on the iPad

1. Go to **Settings, General**, and tap **Bluetooth**
2. Under Bluetooth, tap the **On/Off** Slider and turn on.

Step 2: Pairing the Bluetooth audio device with the iPad. Pairing two Bluetooth devices will have specifics unique to each device, so I will not be able to give you more than a broad overview. In general, though, the process is as follows:

1. Both devices need to be on, and within range of each other. The closer the better, no more than 30 feet, but I would put them within a foot.
2. The iPad's Bluetooth needs to be on
3. The Bluetooth audio device needs to be in discovery mode. In discovery mode, the device says to the world - via Bluetooth, of course - that it is out there and wants to pair with something.
4. On the iPad, the Bluetooth audio device should show up under the device list as **Not Paired**. Tap on it to start the pairing process.
5. The iPad will ask you for a unique number to confirm the pair. This number is in the documents that came with the Bluetooth audio device. Sometimes the

pairing is an automatic process, but other times you will have enter the number on the iPad. When finished, pairing will be complete and the device in the list will state it is Not connected or Connect. If not connected, tap on the text Not Connected and it will then connect.

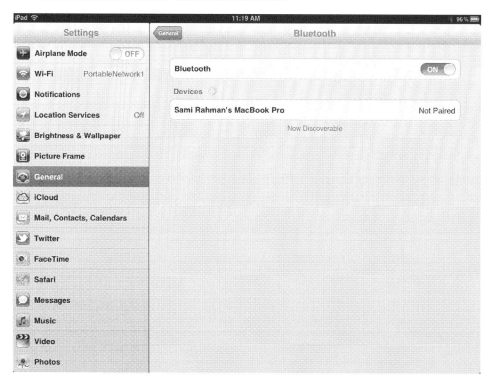

Screenshot of Bluetooth Device List

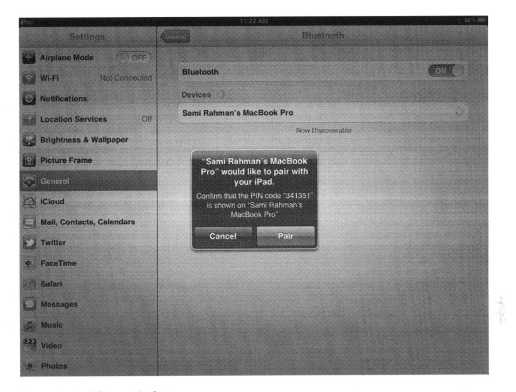

Screenshot of Pair with iPad

Mono Audio

The iPad can route both right- and left-channel audio source material into both earbuds, enabling users with hearing loss in one ear to hear both channels in either ear.

How to Activate Mono Audio

To activate mono audio:

1. Go to **Settings**, **General**, and tap on **Accessibility**
2. Under **Hearing,** tap the Mono Audio **On/Off** slider to turn on
3. Use the L (Left)/ R (Right) slider to select the amount of audio to mix in from either side. In the middle the mix will be 50% audio from both the right and left sides. If you want one to be more dominant than the other, then adjust accordingly.

Screenshot of Mono Audio Setup

Messages with iMessage

With iOS5, Apple created its own messaging system called iMessage™. With iMessage you can text message and send media to anyone on the iMessage system or to anyone using an iPhone. This is all done via wi-fi networks or data plans rather than through the telecommunication companies' text plans, so it is much cheaper and on wi-fi it is free. This can be a good way to communicate for a text based user.

 Tip: iMessage Can Be Free, Normal Texting Can Cost You. If you are new to instant messages AND both users have Apple products, you can use iMessage for free over a wi-fi network. If you use it over a 3G network, you will be charged a data fee, but not the full texting fees most telecommunication companies charge, so it can be very inexpensive. If, however, you are an avid instant message user, you will likely have a number of different services you already use any may not want yet another system.

How to Set Up iMessage for the First Time

To set up and activate iMessage for the first time you will need to do two things - turn iMessage on and set up your iMessage account:

How to turn iMessage on:

1. Go to **Settings**, **Messages** and tap on the **ON/Off** Slider to turn on

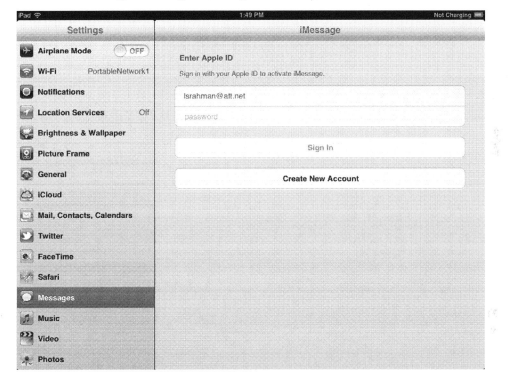

Screenshot of iMessage Default View

How to setup your iMessage account:

1. Go to **Settings**, **Message**, tap **Create New Account**. This can also be done inside the iMessage app as well.

To create an iMessage Account, you will have to provide the following information:

1. First Name
2. Last Name
3. Valid Email Address

4. Password
5. Security Question of your choosing
6. Answer to the Security Question

 Notes:

1. Your iMessage account does not need to be your Apple ID, although it can be,
2. Your account can be the same account you use for other Apple services such as FaceTime
3. You do need to have access to the email account you use, as Apple will send you a confirmation email that you must validate before you can use iMessage
4. First Name, Last Name and email address are searchable by anyone on iMessage.

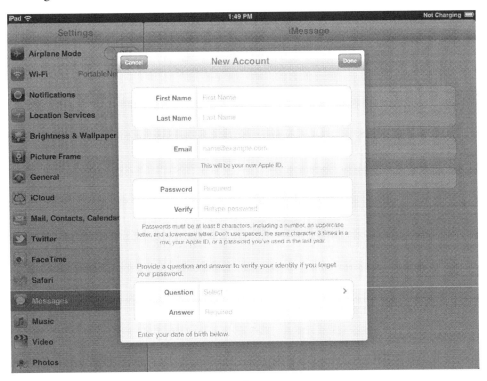

Screenshot of iMessage create new account form

Visual Alerts

There are a lot different options when it comes to visual notifications on an iPad. With iOS5, all application notifications have been streamlined into one system and can be viewed in the Notification Center. The Notification Center is available any time on the iPad by placing your finger on the top of the screen and swiping downward. You can choose on a per app basis how you want to be notified either via Notification Center or a visual alert in the middle of the screen that requires further action.   You can organize the order in which app notifications appear in the Notification Center. This level of control will allow you customize and determine exactly how you want the device to alert you, all based on your preferences, needs, and priorities.

Screenshot of Notifications or Alert popup

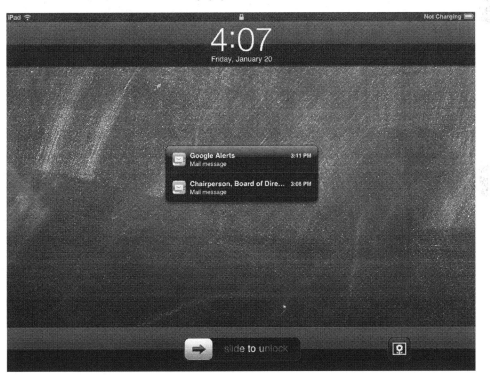

Screenshot of Notifications on Lock Screen

How to Set Up and Edit Notifications

To customize how your notifications work, follow these steps:

1. Go to **Settings**, tap **Notifications**.
2. Go to the app you want to customize and tap on its name
3. Tap on the Notification On/Off Slider to turn it on
4. Under the show option, decide how many items you want to show, 1, 5, 10 or 20 items
5. Alert Styles: There are three styles

   - None - No alert at all, the notification will be in the Notification Center, but not provide any visual alert.

   - Banner - a small alert will drop down as a visual alert

   - Alerts - A message will appear in the middle of the screen and require some sort of action to be taken to remove it. Typically, the action is to select OK or cancel

6. **Badge App Icon:** this controls whether or not you get that little red circle with a message count in the upper right hand corner of the app icon. Think unread mail count.
7. **Show Preview** controls the preview of, for example, an email message in your notification center
8. **View in Lock Screen:** This setting allows you to choose whether or not a notification will show up on the lock screen. This allows you to check notifications you select without having to fully unlock the device.

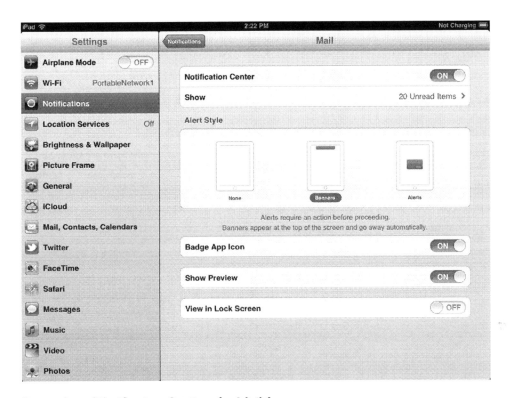

Screenshot of Notifications Settings for Mail App

You can choose in what order your notifications appear in the Notification Center:

1. Go to **General** and tap on **Notifications**
2. Under **Sort Apps** you can choose:

   - **By Time**, which will order the notifications as they come in

   - **Manually** (default)

3. To edit the order, select **Manually** and tap on the edit button in the upper right hand corner. Once in edit mode, you can tap and drop an app up or down the list to reorder.

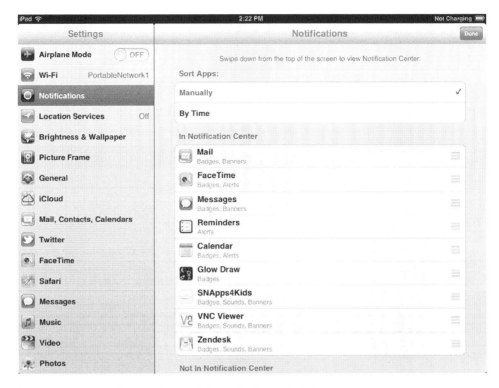

Screenshot of Notification Sort By Manually in Edit Mode

Physical and Motor Skills List

Under the Physical and Motor Skills category, Apple includes the following features:

1. Thin, Light Design
2. Large Muti-Touch Display
3. Tactile Buttons
4. Multiple Orientations
5. Intelligent Onscreen Keyboard with Predictive¬†Text Entry
6. External Keyboards
7. Apple Stereo Headset Compatibility
8. Assistive Touch
9. Sync Automatically

Thin, Light Design

The iPad's design is a very lightweight and durable. Depending upon the needs of the user, you can add cases to suit many different requirements from ruggedness to clamping to a wheelchair.

Photo of Side of iPad (30 pin connector at bottom)

Large Multi-Touch Display

The iPad has a very large 9.7 inch touch-sensitive display. The display does not require any pressure and can be activated by hand, via a mouth stick, head pointer or a custom stylus.

iPad 1 Screen

iPad 2 Screen

Tactile Buttons

The iPad's main buttons are tactile physical buttons. This is important as an accessibility feature in that a lot of technology employs surface touch or "soft" buttons. Soft buttons can be very difficult to use if you do not have good eyesight or fine motor control. While applications on the iPad utilize all sorts of "soft buttons," the fact that the main controls are all tactile physical buttons makes the iPad shine as an accessible device.

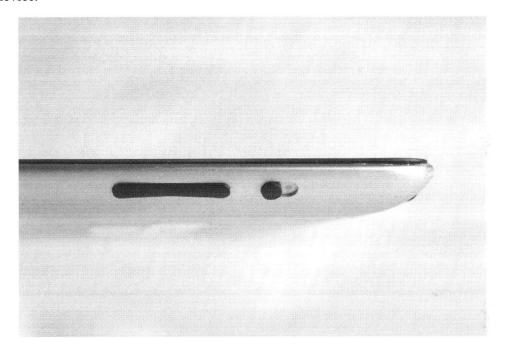

Photo of iPad 2 Volume Rocker and Slider

Multiple Orientations

The iPad can be used in two different orientations, Landscape (sideways) or Portrait modes. It has built-in technology to sense which way the device is oriented and adjust itself accordingly. You can also manually override the sensor and lock it into a fixed position. When the iPad is flat on the table, I have seen some kids struggle with the auto screen rotation. It is reminiscent of seeing a young child putting on a belt. Other kids just seem to ignore it and play games and watch videos upside down. If the auto-rotation becomes a sensory issue, I recommend you lock the screen.

Screenshot of Home Screen with Orientation Lock Enabled

 Tip: If you are having a hard time with the screen rotating all over the place or you want to quickly lock the screen, there is a simple way to do that even if you are in an app. You can do this through the Fast App Switcher:

1. At any point, in an app or on the home screen, double tap the home button. This will bring up the Fast App Switcher.

Screenshot Showing Fast App Switcher Dock (Multitasking Bar)

2. Swipe to the right and you are presented with a few preferences. On the far left side, you will see a button with a circle arrow or the Orientation unlock button. See below

Screenshot showing Lock Screen Orientation unlocked

3. Tap the Orientation unlock button and a closed lock will appear. Now the screen is locked and will not rotate until you unlock it again. The screen will also show a larger orientation status in the middle of the screen.

Screenshot showing Landscape Orientation Locked

4. To unlock, follow these same steps, this time tapping the Orientation button to remove the lock from the icon.

Note: This trick assumes you have the side switch set to mute, which is the default setting. The switch can be reset to lock orientation instead, as described in the next section.

How to Change the Mute Button Into a Screen Rotation Lock Button

If screen rotation is more of an issue for you than putting the iPad into mute mode, then you can choose to change the mute button into a screen rotation lock button. Here's how:

1. Go to **Settings** and tap **General**
2. Under the section called **Use Side Switch to**, tap on **Lock Rotation**. The default is Mute.
3. Once Lock Rotation is selected, you can use the side switch above the volume rocker to lock or unlock the rotation of the screen

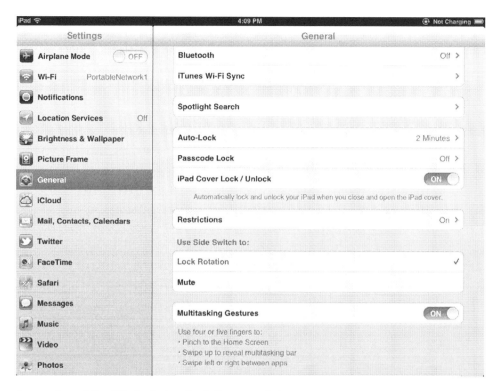

Screenshot of Use Side Switch to Lock Rotation Selected

Intelligent Onscreen Keyboard with Predictive Text Entry

While typing, the iPad uses predictive text technology to help the user reduce the amount of keystrokes needed to create words. The system will learn how you type and will get better as you use it. The system will also will capitalize words it thinks should be in caps and add punctuation to words it thinks are contractions, like I'm or don't.

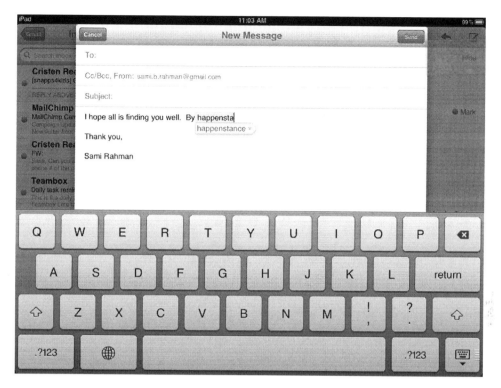

Screenshot of Predictive Text Inside Mail Program

External Keyboards

An external keyboard can be connected via Bluetooth to the iPad for those users who need a more tactile experience. The iPad supports the Apple Wireless Keyboard and most other Bluetooth wireless keyboards using the Apple keyboard layout. This can be a great stepping stone if the onboard screen is not suitable. Or it can be the primary text interface. We use a keyboard with Noah. He likes the feel of the physical keys and seems to be more accurate with them, with fewer miskeys. Other Bluetooth keyboards may work, too, although some unique or specialized keys may not be supported or work as expected.

Photo of External Bluetooth Keyboard.

Tip: We were trying to find a way to differentiate the Arabic keyboard from the English keyboard. At the time Noah was really into hunting and pecking Arabic letters. I found that when we used a laptop, he was very engaged while using the physical keys, but I could not get the same level of engagement when we used an onscreen keyboard. I purchased an external Bluetooth English keyboard and used very inexpensive Arabic keyboard stickers to convert it into an Arabic keyboard. I did this mainly because I could not find a suitable Bluetooth Arabic keyboard. It works well enough that we are considering using it with English and if he learns another language with that new language as well.

Photo Apple Keyboard with Arabic Letter Stickers

Apple Stereo Headset Compatibility

The headphone adapter can be outfitted with a headphone/microphone headset that can be used to record your voice for speech to text applications, or for some applications like Music where you can use voice commands. Voice commands are application specific and most applications will not understand them. That said, I suspect you will see this area of accessibility expand.

Dragon Dictation

Cost: Free
Developer: Nuance Communications
iTunes URL: *http://itunes.apple.com/us/app/dragon-dictation/id341446764?mt=8*

Dragon Dictation has been around on the PC and Mac for a while. It is a speech to text translation device. You speak into the application and it converts the words it hears to text. You can save it, copy and paste into emails, share it, etc.

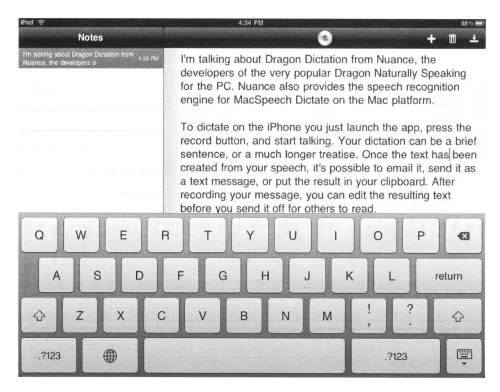

Screenshot of Dragon Dictation

AssistiveTouch

The iPad uses a number of multi-finger, multi-directional gestures to short cut, simplify and navigate the applications and operating system. Some of the gestures can be very difficult for someone with physical impairments to accomplish regularly with any device fluency. Enter AssistiveTouch. AssistiveTouch is an operating system level set of menus that can be used to replace any number of physical gestures or actions. It can also be triggered by a headset or by external switches. This is a very big deal for anyone who may struggle making positive contact with the multitouch screen.

AssistiveTouch is a very extensive set of accessibility features, so let me start by using a simple example to explain. In a number of games and applications, you need to shake the iPad to clear the screen or mix items. This is a very nice way to interact with the device. But if you have a hard time picking up the iPad, or if, for example, it is mounted to a wheelchair, how are you going to be able to shake it? If you have As-sistiveTouch activated, then you can activate the menu, tap on device, tap on "Shake" device. This will then virtually shake the iPad, although there is a caveat to this.

Note: Not all programs work with AssistiveTouch. Experiment. It seems that the programs must be written to utilize AssistiveTouch commands, so those that do not will not respond to the AssistiveTouch commands. It is likely that a number of programs that don't work with AssistiveTouch will get updates, so periodically check. Don't just discount an app if it does not work with AssistiveTouch at the moment.

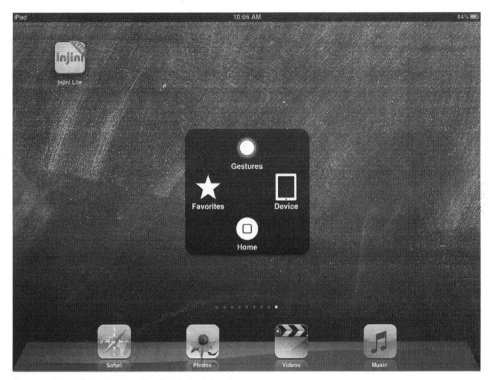

Screenshot of Assistive Touch Main Menu.

AssistiveTouch Menu Breakdown

In iOS 5, AssistiveTouch's main menu consists of four buttons:

1. **Home** - This works just like tapping on the physical home button
2. **Gestures** - This button accesses the gestures sub-menu which allows you to do a number of multi-finger gestures with one tap
3. **Device** - This button accesses the device sub-menu which allows you to control physical

AssistiveTouch Main Menu

buttons on the iPad

4. **Favorites** - This button accesses the favorites sub-menu where you can trigger custom gestures.
5. **Center of the main menu** - There is no icon but if you tap here it will deactivate a custom gesture if you have selected one. (See Custom Gesture section)

The AssistiveTouch Gesture sub-menu has 5 buttons:

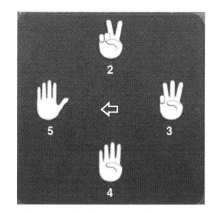

1. **Left Facing Arrow.** The back button, tap here to take you back to the main menu.
2. **2-5 multi-finger icons.** Selecting the number of fingers you want to use on screen at once will put that many blue virtual fingers on screen. Using just a single tap and drop, you can simulate a gesture in whatever direction you move with as many fingers as you have selected.

AssistiveTouch Gesture Sub-menu

The AssistiveTouch Device sub-menu has 6 buttons and 1 additional sub-menu:

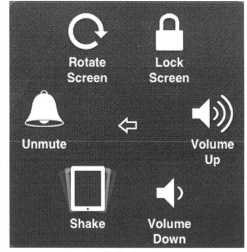

1. **Left Facing Arrow** - The back button, tap here to take you back to the main menu.
2. **Rotate Screen** - See Rotate Screen sub-menu
3. **Lock Screen** - Puts the iPad into lock screen mode
4. **Mute/UnMute** - Toggle
5. **Volume Up** - Turn volume up 1 step for every tap
6. **Shake** - Virtually shake the iPad.
7. **Volume Down** - Turn volume down 1 step for every tap

AssistiveTouch Device Sub-menu

The AssistiveTouch Rotate Screen has 5 buttons:

1. **Left Facing Arrow** - The back button, tap here to take you back to the main menu.

2. **Portrait** - Rotate Screen to portrait orientation
3. **Left** - Rotate Screen to the Left
4. **Right** - Rotate Screen to the Right
5. **Upside Down** - Rotate Screen Upside Down

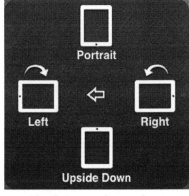

Note: When you use each of the rotation buttons, the rotation is relative to where the iPad screen is currently oriented. Tap the left button 4 times and you will go all the way around 360 degrees.

Note: Screen rotation and screen rotation lock are dependent. So if you rotate the screen using AssistiveTouch, and screen rotation lock is not set, it will not stay in the same position if you move the iPad.

AssistiveTouch Rotate Screen Sub-menu

The AssistiveTouch Gesture sub-menu has 9 buttons:

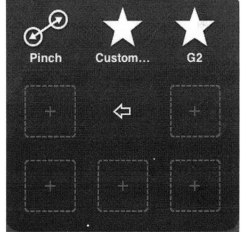

1. **Left Facing Arrow** - The back button, tap here to take you back to the main menu.
2. **Pinch** - Default Pinch Gesture
3. There are 7 empty slots for custom gestures (seen here with 2 custom gestures created)

Important Note: Once a custom gesture is selected, it will remain active until you deactivate the gesture. To deactivate a gesture, open the AssistiveTouch main menu and tap in the center in between the buttons.

AssistiveTouch Favorites Sub-menu

How to Activate AssistiveTouch

To activate AssistiveTouch, follow these steps:

1. Go to **Settings**, **General**, **Accessibility** and tap on **AssistiveTouch**.
2. Tap the AssistiveTouch **On/Off** Slider to activate AssistiveTouch. The default is Off
3. Once AssistiveTouch is active, a small white button on a dark gray transparent background will appear on screen and will be there in all apps. You can move it

by tapping and dragging, but it will snap to the closest edge in 1 of 8 positions: all four corners, the 1/3rd and 2/3rd position left and right. This is awkward to describe, so just play around with it; it is easy to use and move.

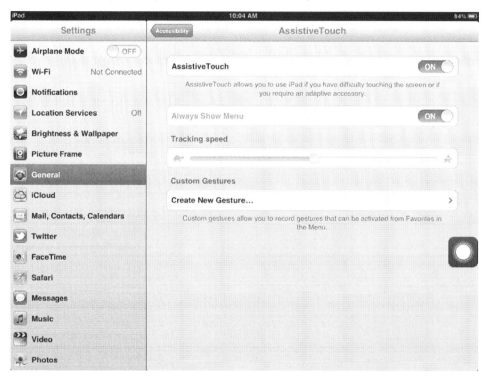

Screenshot of AssistiveTouch Setting Screen

Custom Gestures

Under the AssistiveTouch menu item in **Settings**, **General**, **Accessibility**, you will find **Create Custom Gesture**. This is a very interesting feature that I did not understand at first. I thought it was going to be some way to program the iPad with custom commands. That is not it. Rather, it is a way to create a short cut to gestures that already exist in the system but that you want to trigger using the AssistiveTouch menu. Let me explain by using a simple example.

Let's say you read a lot and want to scroll down a page at a time, but don't want to have to tap and drag all of the time. With custom gestures, you can record a single finger swipe down the page and name it something meaningful like "scroll down." Assuming you are in iBook or Safari, or wherever you do a lot of reading and Assistive-Touch is activated, you will find under the favorites button your "scroll down" custom gesture. Tap on it and from now on the default action will be your custom gesture when you swipe the screen. So now you when you want to scroll down, a single finger swipe down the screen will page down, do it again and down you go and so forth. To deactivate, launch the AssistiveTouch menu and tap dead center in the menu, this will deactivate the custom gesture and return you to normal use.

The custom gesture feature can implemented to simplify the triggering of complex or repetitive gestures for any user. This can reduce frustration and increase efficiency for not only a special needs user but anyone. It does take some getting used to and experimentation to get the most out of the feature and for some there may not be any need for it at all.

How to Create a Custom Gesture

To create custom gestures, follow these steps:

1. In **Settings**, under **General**, under **Accessibility** under **AssistiveTouch**, tap **Create New Gesture**.

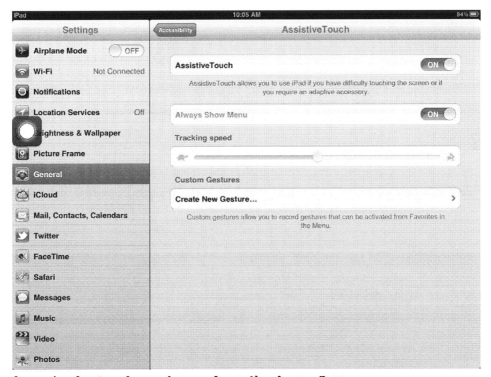

Screenshot Settings, Custom Gesture, Create New Gesture Button

2. Using the **New Gesture** work area (blank area in the middle of the screen),

drag your hand across the screen to create any custom gesture you want. In most cases, the user will be creating the gesture that is most appropriate for them. In the example I will do a 3 finger downward gesture.

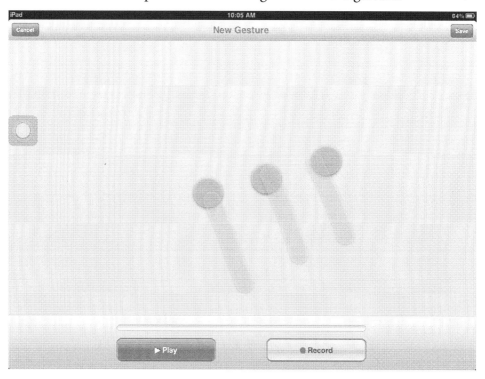

Screenshot of Custom Gesture Record Area While Recording Gesture.

3. Once done, tap the stop button at the bottom
4. To save, tap the "Save" button in the upper right hand corner
5. Name your custom gesture. I recommend very short and meaningful names. No more than 6 characters will show up in the AssistiveTouch Menu.

Screenshot of Save Custom Gesture

Once you are have created your custom gesture, it will appear in the AssistiveTouch menu under gestures.

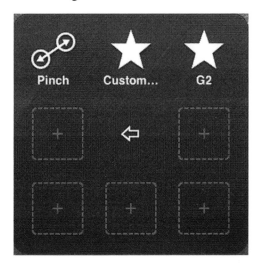

Screenshot of Custom Gesture in AssistiveTouch Menu

Activate and Deactivate Custom Gestures

In order to use custom gestures, you need to have AssistiveTouch turned on. You also need to create a custom gesture and save it to the iPad.

To activate a custom gesture:

1. Tap on the AssistiveTouch on screen menu button
2. Tap the Favorites icon
3. Tap the custom gesture you would like to activate

Note: The gesture will be the default action when you touch the screen until you deactivate the gesture.

To deactivate a custom gesture:

1. Tap on the AssistiveTouch on-screen menu button
2. Tap dead center (blank area of menu between all buttons). This action deactivates the custom gesture.

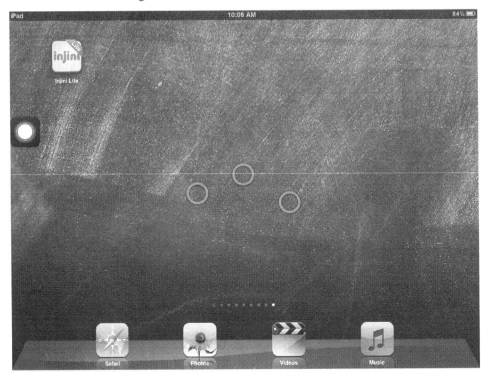

Screenshot of Using Custom Gesture from AssistiveTouch menu

Sync Automatically

Automatically Sync uses a wi-fi connection instead of the sync cable to sync the iPad to iTunes. This can reduce the need to attach cables, mouse clicks and process management. The really nice thing is that once it is set up, it is automatic so you don't need to manage it, it just happens. Automatic Sync can sync the following items:

1. Applications
2. Media - TV, Movies, Podcasts, Music, iTunes U, Photos
3. Books
4. Contacts
5. Calendars
6. Bookmarks
7. Notes
8. Ringtones

How to Set Up Automatic Sync

To set up Automatic Sync, follow these steps:

1. Launch iTunes on the computer.
2. Attach the iPad to the computer via the sync cable
3. In iTunes, in the left hand menu click on the iPad to reveal the Summary page
4. Under **Options**, select **Sync with iTunes over Wi-Fi**
5. Click **Apply**.

Screenshot of How to Setup Automatic Sync via Wi-Fi in iTunes

 Note: For the iPad to automatically sync with iTunes, the following must be true:

1. The iPad is plugged into a power source
2. iTunes is open on a computer and the computer is awake
3. iTunes and iPad are on the same Wi-Fi network

CHAPTER

Introduction to Communi-cation on the iPad

One of the most highlighted areas where the iPad has affected the special needs community is its ability to act as a very cost effective communication device, along with its impact on the world of Augmentative Alternative Communication, or AAC. It is often the reason parents buy an iPad for their special needs children. As we all know, buying a device alone will not allow anyone to just magically communicate, communication is about implementing the right strategy for the user and then supporting them through the process. Typically, children do not learn to communicate overnight, and neither do special needs users of any age. The following chapter will cover the basics of communication strategies, how to implement them using the iPad and some of the many apps you might try. I have seen it with my own eyes - the iPad can be a very effective tool in your communication arsenal. It is relatively inexpensive, is not intimidating for non-AAC users, and its multipurpose-ness enables the user to employ it in many ways. In other words, it has the ability to be many different types of AAC devices rolled into one.

What is AAC?

AAC stands for Augmentative Alternative Communication. AAC is a category of speech therapy that brings together both assistive technology, both low and high tech, and communication strategies to help those who do not communicate typically. This subcategory of special needs is a whole universe in and of itself, so for the sake of this book I am providing a brief overview.

AAC software and the underlying strategy can be broken down into two main categories: symbol-based communication and text-to-speech based. This is logical - if a person does not read or understand text, then it would not be beneficial for them to have a program that would speak the text typed into the iPad. This is where symbol-based communication comes into play. As we all have heard, a picture is worth a thousand words, so using something as simple as having two pictures and getting the user to indicate which of the two pictures they want can be an effective way for the user to make a choice. Indicating choice is one of the primary and fundamental purposes of communication. String a few pictures together and now you have a sentence.

This is the concept behind PECs, or Picture Exchange Communication. Learning and using a PEC system can be a very effective way to communicate in and of itself, and be the basis of and entry ramp to text-based communication. Of course, it all depends on the user and the support system around the user.

Symbol-Based Communication Systems

A very effective and low-tech method for symbol-based communication is a choice board. It is a card, usually laminated or otherwise protected. It may have a few words, like "yes" and "no," and a number of pictures. The user points to what they want. It is very effective, does not require batteries, and does not have a steep learning curve. Because it can be created specifically for the user, it can have large pictures for those with fine motor difficulties, or can have custom pictures for those who need to see an object exactly as it is in their world in order to relate to it.

Text-Based Communication Systems

Text-based communication systems are those systems that use text instead of pictures as the primary input mechanism. The text that is entered by the user is then converted to speech by the computer system. You will often see this category of communication referred to as text-to-speech Communication. Unlike low-tech systems, text-to-speech requires a computer to complete the process. There are some very effective devices that will record speech and trigger it based on the push of a button. However, they do not do this conversion on the fly, so you would not be able to type in a unique line of text and have the machine read it out loud. On the other end of the spectrum of text-to-speech, though, there are systems that do just that - convert text into speech on the fly - that can be used on cell phones, portable computers, desktop computers, etc.

Text-to-speech requires the user to understand written language and, depending upon the application interface, may also require a high degree of fine motor control for use on a cell phone keypad, for example. This is why you typically do not start with text-based communication systems.

Getting Started with AAC

You cannot just put an iPad with Proloquo2Go (a symbol-based communication app that is one of the more advanced symbol-based apps on the market) in front of a user and hope they get it. For any user, learning to communicate period, whether or not they have an impairment, is a long process. It follows that there should be a learning process when using augmentative alternative communication as well. Here are the main considerations:

1. How will your user adapt to the iPad?
2. Where do you start with them?

   - What skills do they already have?

   - What skills do they need to build?

3. What are your short-term communication goals?
4. What are your long-term communication goals?

Every user will have their own unique path regarding communication. I cannot stress enough how important having professionals like Speech and Language Pathologists, Assistive Technology specialists, and Special Education Teachers on your team will be. Executing a communication plan can take years; having a professional to assist you can dramatically shorten that path.

How Will Your User Adapt to the iPad?

No matter if communication is your first goal or a subsequent goal in using the iPad, you will have to start getting your user accustomed to the iPad itself. Depending upon your user's skill level, you may have to plan to spend some time with them getting familiar with the iPad and building basic skills before stepping into serious communication work. This is not to say that you cannot use basic "yes/no" apps or a PECs based "I Want" app to get them started expressing choices and preferences. The key will be to get the iPad to engage your user in a way that is meaningful to them. For some users, this can be simply having fun with the iPad; to others, meaning will only come through using the iPad as a communication device. I can only imagine how frustrating it would be to want to communicate with others and not be able to do so. The message here is that step 1 is to engage your user in a manner that is meaningful to them and make the iPad usable for them.

Where Do You Start?

Start with an assessment. You will need to assess your user's current skills and skill levels.

1. In what fashion do they currently communicate? Grunt and point, PECs, words? Once you know your starting point, you will build from there.
2. What other factors are at play here - sensory, oral motor, spectrum? What obstacles do you anticipate you will have to address and/or overcome?
3. What skills exist already?
4. What skills need to be developed?

What Are Your Short-Term Communication Goals?

What are your short-term goals? Where to start will vary, depending on your user and their immediate goals. Examples of short-term goals that I have seen for AAC users getting started:

1. Using an index finger (i.e., finger isolation) to indicate Yes or No: Yes (big green button) and No (big red button) on the iPad
2. Indicate a choice among 3 foods for a meal. Using a symbol-based communication app, select the words "I Want," then select among 3 pictures of breakfast foods.

The key to the short-term goal will be to make the experience meaningful for the user. The ability to express preferences around meal time, for example, is a very powerful experience for an individual who has not been able to do so easily before. I know of a parent who used an iPad with their child for a very long time before they got all of the pieces together to use an AAC app, but once they did, they did something with their 4 year old within a day that they had never done before - find out what he wanted for breakfast. They gave him 3 pictures of items and he was able to select the one he wanted on the iPad. How powerful is that? It gives me goose bumps just typing it.

What Are Your Long-Term Communication Goals?

Long-term goals around communication usually involve freely interacting with the outside world. In other words, independent communication within and outside of the immediate circle of caregivers. I have seen the iPad used as a long-term communication device, as well as seen it used as a stepping stone to a Dynavox, which is a highly customizable device designed specifically as an AAC device. It is also safe to say that as the user progresses and develops, your long term goals will change. They key message is that your long-term goals can affect how you approach your short-term goals so you should spend some time understanding what the long-term landscape could be and how you can build towards that now.

Yes/No Communication Apps

Yes/No communication apps do precisely what their name implies - they give you two buttons, a big green button with the word "Yes," and a big red button with the word "No." Select the option you want after being presented with a question and the app will say your answer for you. For a number of new users, this is their first AAC app. There are no libraries of pictures to scroll through, nor is there lots of complicated mechanics to navigate. It is very straight-forward. What is significant about using this kind of app is not the yes/no element, as a finger point and grunt can usually get you to the same goal, it is that you are establishing a universal pattern for communication that is easily replicated. That is, you ask a question and present two choices to the user, then they get to select, or respond to you. This cycle of communication is universal no matter what form of communication you use. What you are really doing is reinforcing this universal cycle, which you will build upon later as your methods of communication advance.

Answers:YesNo HD

Cost: $4
Developer: SimplifiedTouch
iTunes URL: *http://itunes.apple.com/us/app/answers-yesno-hd/id393762442?mt=8*

Answers: YesNo HD is designed to provide a user with a very simple method for communicating binary information. That is, Yes or No. Press a button and it will say your answer, communicating your choice to others. Within the program you have the ability to create up to 30 custom pages with your own binary choices. You can make a recording of each choice so when you select it, the choice will be communicated verbally as well.

Screenshot of Answers:YesNo HD

 Tip: Answer Yes No is a great starting program for both new users to the iPad and new users to AAC. It is simple to use and understand. It can give a user an effective voice very quickly.

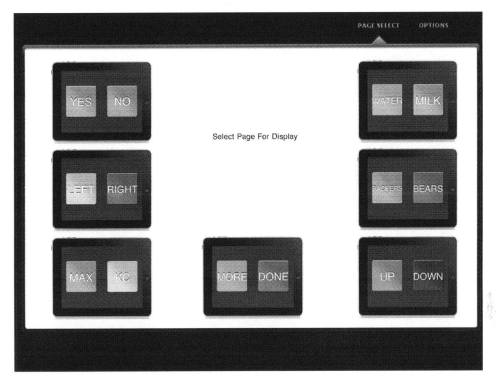

Second Screenshot showing Alternate Pairings of Answers:YesNo HD

My Choice Board - Symbol Based

My Choice Board was designed by the parents of an autistic child who wanted a way for their child to communicate preferences. Seeking an app that was simple, easy to use and intuitive to set up, they created My Choice Board. It is one of the very first apps we at BridgingApps.org recommend that people start with when they want to use the iPad as an AAC device. It is simple and effective for both the parent/caregiver and the user.

The program works using the metaphor of a clip board. Each clip is an organization group, for example, Play Games. On each clipboard you have a selection of items from which to choose. Once an item is selected, it will say that item aloud for you and you then get a very large version (picture) of the item on screen.

Here is what it looks like to use the App

1. Select the clipboard you want to use and present it to the user.
2. Allow the user to select the item they want. Once the item is selected it will

play the pre-recorded audio clip and show you a large version of the image.

My Choice Board

Cost: $10
Developer: Good Karma Applications, Inc.
iTunes URL: *http://itunes.apple.com/us/app/my-choice-board/id384435705?mt=8*

The primary purpose of My Choice Board is to present a visual display of "choices" to those with limited communication skills. This gives individuals with autism, communication delays or learning differences the opportunity to be independent and express their own specific needs and wants.

Screenshots of My Choice Board

Tips: Here are a few tips and tricks when using My Choice Boards:

1. My Choice Boards is a great way to start a user on the path of AAC. The "I Want" plus choices set up can be customized to be any motivator that works for your user. This makes it very flexible for a variety of ages, cognitive ability, etc.

2. Create a board based on a meal preference or treat, or a favorite toy
3. Use it as a method of selecting a reward.
4. My Choice Board was not made for ad hoc communication, though. It was designed to have the clip boards created in advance.
5. Having a camera on board makes creating new icons easy
6. Polish off your singing voice as you will likely be the vocal talent.
7. Consider having a version on your iPhone, or an iTouch to use on the go when the iPad is not accessible.

My First AAC

My First AAC was designed as an augmentative alternative communications app for toddlers and preschoolers. The symbols and layout are designed to be more toddler and kid friendly than Proloquo2Go, for example, which has some symbols that are geared more for adult and more cognitively developed users. This application is a good introduction to AAC apps for very young users who would benefit from a more simple interface.

My First AAC
Cost: $25
Developer: NCsoft
iTunes URL: *http://itunes.apple.com/us/app/my-first-aac/id462678851?mt=8*

This is an AAC app specifically designed for toddlers. It has more meaningful symbols and interface designed for toddlers and preschoolers. It can also be a starter AAC app for cognitively challenged older users to help them develop basic AAC skills.

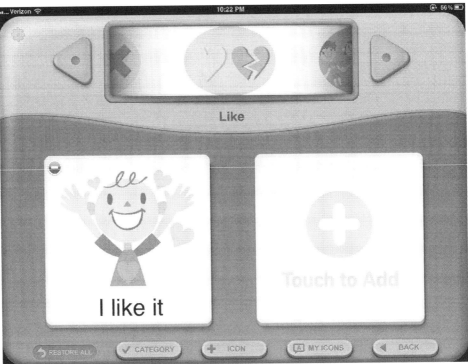

Screenshots of My First AAC

Speak It! - Text to Speech

Speak It! is a text-to-speech application - type in text and it will repeat what you have typed. You can select different voices. It has the ability to save phrases in a list to reuse later. And you can even save phrases to an audio file that you can email to someone to keep in the list. Unlike a full blown AAC app, however, there is only one list, and it cannot be sub-divided. For this reason, I think of this app as being better suited for ad hoc communication. Speak It! can also be used to read documents and email aloud.

As this is a text-to-speech app, the user has to be able to spell what they want and have the dexterity and fine motor skills to do so. This rules out a lot of users, so it would not be suitable as a starter app. However, if you already have these skills, talking could become as simple as texting, and that can allow for freedom in communication.

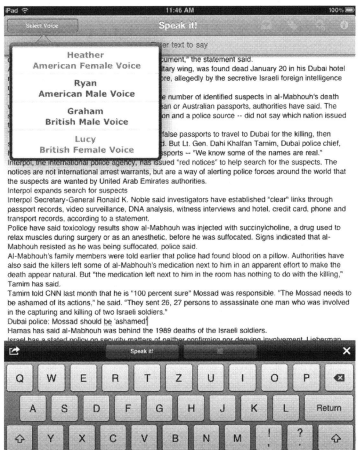

Speak it! Screenshot: Entering Text to be Spoken

Speak it! Screenshot: List of Saved Phrases and Audio Files

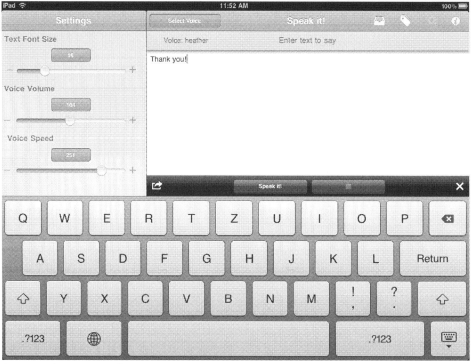

Speak it! Screenshot: Phrase Settings Editor

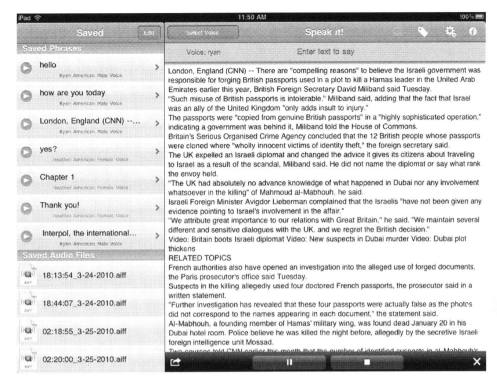

Speak it! Screenshot: Reading a Document Back to You

Speak It!

Cost: $2

Developer: Future Apps Inc.

iTunes URL: http://itunes.apple.com/us/app/speak-it-text-to-speech/id308629295?mt=8

Introducing Speak it! 2, the most advanced text to speech solution in the App Store! Speak it has now been designed to work with iOS 4, and take advantage of all the multitasking features.

Proloquo2Go

Proloquo2Go is a symbol-based alternative augmentative communication app that was originally developed for the iPhone/iPod Touch. When the iPad was released, it found an even greater audience. It is based around the concept of using symbols to build phrases, as you build phrases the device will then speak them for you. You can store and trigger words, sentences and more. You can develop libraries of related words and phrases for later use, or use the built in library of thousands of words and phrases on the fly, whatever works best for the user.

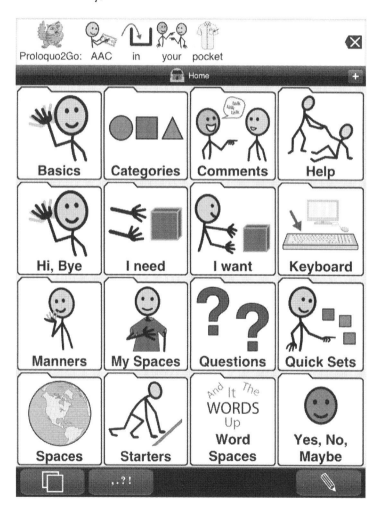

Screenshot of Proloquo2Go Breakfast Folder with "I want" Phrase and Different Breakfast Items

To better illustrate how Proloquo2Go works, let's take the simple example of having breakfast each morning. For someone who is not verbal, how can they communicate to you what they want to eat? Below is a screenshot of a simple breakfast page; the first icon the left represents the concept of "I want." The user would select (touch) that button. Notice at the top of the screen you have a sentence bar and you can see the words "I want" and "Yogurt." You can see that both the "I want" and "Yogurt" buttons were selected. As they were selected, the application said "I want" and then "Yogurt." Also note that the picture of the yogurt is an actual picture. This can be very meaningful for certain users. With an iPad 2 or iPhone/iPod Touch, you can take pictures of actual objects and add them. For iPad 1 users, you can download pictures from the web or take a picture with a camera and transfer it to the iPad using iTunes.

Proloquo2Go is more than a simple "I want" or touch board program, however. It is an interactive app. Proloquo2Go comes with thousands of words and phrases as part of the app. It was designed to be used both in the pre-configured way and in an on-the-fly interactive manner. See the screen below, which is the home screen of Proloquo2Go from the teacher in my son's special needs school. The default home screen would not include the "Student pages," "School," and "Fashion show" folders. These are custom folders created by the teacher to better organize and serve her needs. Note the standard folders like "Basics," "Categories," "Comments," "Demo," and "Help". The words and phrases that are standard with the program are in these folders.

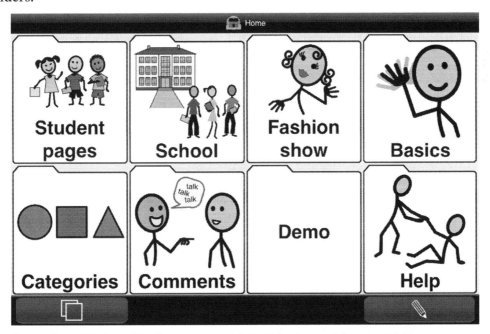

Screenshot of Proloquo2Go Home screen with Both Custom and Standard Folders

Proloquo2Go

Cost: $200
Developer: AssistiveWare
iTunes URL: *http://itunes.apple.com/us/app/proloquo2go/id308368164?mt=8*

Proloquo2Go provides a full-featured augmentative and alternative communication solution for people who have difficulty speaking. It provides natural sounding text-to-speech voices (CURRENTLY AMERICAN, BRITISH and INDIAN ENGLISH ONLY), high resolution up-to-date symbols, powerful automatic conjugations, a default vocabulary of over 7000 items, advanced word prediction, full expandability and extreme ease of use.

Editing and Adding New Words in Proloquo2Go

While this is not designed to be a tutorial on Proloquo2Go, I did want to show you how easy it is to create and edit folders and words or phrases in Proloquo2Go for two reasons: first, it is how most Symbol-to-Text programs work, and, second, Proloquo2Go is the top application in the category.

You can start editing anywhere. For the sake of this tutorial, we will start with the breakfast screen. Let's say I want to edit the Drink button.

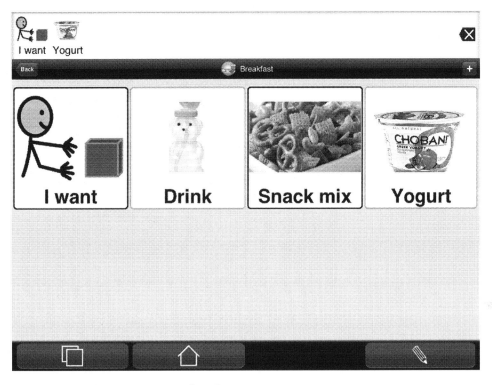

Screenshot of Proloquo2go Breakfast Page

I would start by click on the pencil button in the lower right corner of the page; this puts Proloquo2Go into edit mode. When the app is in edit mode, the background turns from gray to blue.

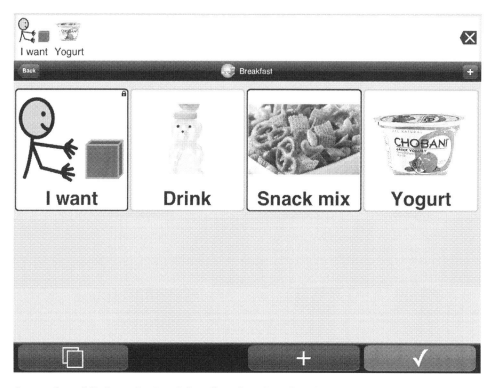

Screenshot of Proloquo2go Breakfast Page Edit Note Turn On

Once in edit mode, touch your finger to the screen on the icon you want to edit and hold it there until the edit menu appears.

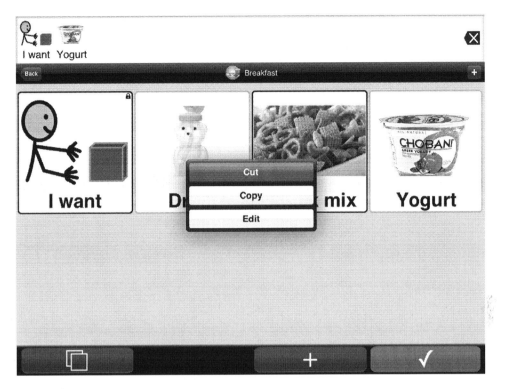

Screenshot of Proloquo2go Breakfast Page Editing an Item

Once the edit menu appears, select "Edit." Also note, you can select "Cut" to remove the icon or "Copy." Copy is important because it allows you to create an icon once and move or copy it to many different pages. A good example of this is the "I Want" icon.

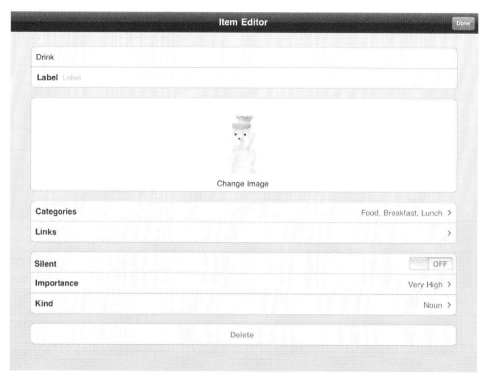

Screenshot of Proloquo2go Item Editor for "Drink" Icon

Now you will find yourself in the Item Editor. Here you can change any of the icon's attributes. For example, I can change the icon picture by touching the icon picture long enough for the Picture Options menu to pop up.

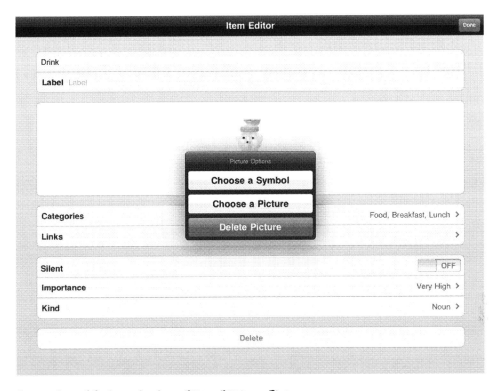

Screenshot of Proloquo2go Item Editor, Editing a Picture

In the Picture Options menu, you can see that I can select "Delete Picture", or "Choose a Symbol" from the Proloquo2Go library or "Choose a Picture" from the photo library on the iPad.

Screenshot of Proloquo2go Item Editor, Editing a Picture, Selecting Picture from Photo Library

I have selected **Choose a Picture** button, it then opens a box to allow me to select a photo from any found in my photo library.

Categories and Links:

It can help to think of categories as pages and links as folders. For the example we have been using, the icon (Item) is "Drink," which you have seen on the Breakfast page. In Proloquo2go, the category would be "Breakfast." If you want to add a folder on the Breakfast page called "Drink," you would change the Links field to include the Breakfast Category. You would then see the "Drink" icon change to a "Drink" folder.

 Tip: Here are a numbers of items to keep in mind when you are first getting started with Proloquo2Go:

1. Keep it very simple. If your user is new to the iPad, which is likely, and they are new to symbol-based or PECS based communication systems, then you really need to keep the choices down to a minimum. Consider creating a page with just YES and No and don't use any other page for a while.

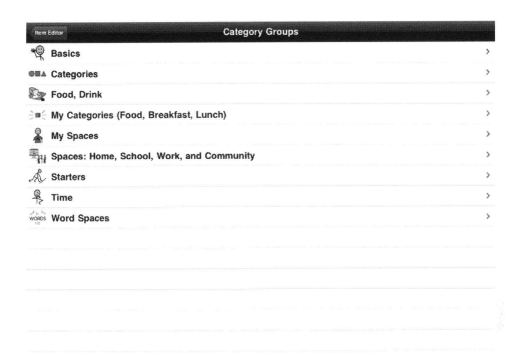

Screenshot of Proloquo2go Category Groups

2. Consider using a simpler program to get them started, such as My Choice Board.

3. Consider starting with simple choices, like 2 or 3 items for a meal with the "I want" button.

4. Clean your home screen: Depending upon your user's ability to navigate and comprehend the layout of the folders and pages, you may want simplify the home screen. Create a new folder on the home page, then put all of the other folders into the new folder. Call it something meaningful like "Library," then create new folders and pages that are meaningful to your user.

5. Think and plan for Proloquo2Go to be a learning and developmental process. Start with goals like simple usage and work up to more complex tasks, like having a full conversation. This is especially important to new users to symbol-based communication.

AAC Checklist

User Checklist

1. Is the user already training on a communication system?

    -   PECs?

    -   Text-to-Speech?

2. What Communication training do they need and how will it be reinforced? (i.e., in school, at home, in public, etc.)
3. What is your plan for acclimating to the iPad before you start AAC app usage?
4. What impairments, if any, will you have to plan for - fine motor, cognitive, attention, sensory, etc.?

Hardware Checklist

1. iPad
2. Case
3. Screen protector
4. Keyguard, if so for what apps
5. Any other accessories, e.g. stylus, mounting brackets, holders, home button protector

Software Checklist

1. What apps are you going to use as introduction to AAC on the iPad, i.e., starting point?
2. What are some of the various apps you going to use to develop skills? This may include non-AAC apps as well.
3. What are your long-term goals? For example, you may want your users to use Proloquo2Go as a long-term communication system.

CHAPTER

Getting the Most from Your iPad

After you get comfortable and spend some time with your iPad, you will likely want to do more with it and you will want to do it more easily. In this chapter we will cover:

1. Searching for Apps
2. Testing and Removing Apps
3. Creating your own content
4. Things you should know about iPad buttons

Finding and Buying Apps

There are a number of ways to find apps. You can use your computer to do an internet search, use iTunes, or use the App Store on your iPad. We will cover all three and talk about a few apps that may help you find apps as well. Keep in mind that there are over 500,000 apps in the App Store published by over 121,000 developers. There are almost 50,000 apps in the educational category alone. So the question really is not "are there apps out there?" The question is "how do I find the right app for my situation?"

The short answer, once you understand a little terminology and become familiar with how apps work, is that it really is a matter of focusing on the skills you want to address and experimenting. Skills, skills, skills. Did I says skills yet? Let me illustrate by example. We were trying to get Noah to move from having his hands in a fist all of the time to using his index finger - in other words, the skill we were looking to develop was finger isolation. We started by searching for "finger isolation" in iTunes, which did not produce any results at the time. We then considered what would make his fingers move in a way that he could not do with his fist. We looked for programs that made him move pieces across the screen. Specifically, we looked for toddler puzzles. We looked for pieces that were small enough to force him to use his finger, but big enough so that he would not get frustrated. We found Monkey Preschool Lunchbox. It had a number of games, one of which was a puzzle. Noah had a very hard time completing them at the start, but the rest of games were so much fun for him that he kept working at the puzzles until he started to get it. He got better and better at them. It look a long time, but he did it.

Searching

Here are the steps I recommend using to find a specific app:

1. Determine the skill needed
2. Search the App Store or iTunes
3. Read the description
4. Look at screenshots
5. Read some of the comments, most of which will not be applicable
6. Go to developer's website and read more extended write-ups
7. Download a lite version
8. Test the app

- Yourself

- With your user

9. Keep or remove the app.

If I don't know, or if I am not sure Noah will like or use the app, I have been known to leave it on his iPad and see if he will discover the app on his own. I will show it to him a couple of times. If after a prolonged period there is really no interest, I will remove it.

Note: It is kind of like a toy - I don't leave all of his toys out at once. I will take away unused toys for a while and then reintroduce them. I also do it to manage space on the home screen. I am not too keen on having have to flip through up to 11 pages.

Note: I test all of the apps before Noah sees them, especially the free/lite apps. I have found a number of them are not what I want for Noah. Or, for example, I found the free/lite version to be half the alphabet and you have to buy the other half. If I like it enough, I will buy the whole thing; otherwise, I test it with Noah and if he likes it, then I'll buy it. My issue it not having to buy the app, my issue is showing him an app I think is complete and him loving it, getting halfway through and it not moving to the next letter. Big conflict in our house that day. He was not happy, I was not happy. The worst thing was that I was happy to buy the rest of the program, but the in app upgrade did not work and there was no full version in the App Store. Very big conflict in our house that day indeed.

Understanding What You Are Buying When You Buy Apps

When you purchase an app, whether for money or download it for free, you are "buying" the right to use the app with any device tied to your account (some limitations do apply). You are also buying that app and all future versions of it, so if they upgrade the app, you will get a new copy, provided you keep your device updated. You can even remove an app from your iPad and at a later date re-install the latest version of it. All of this information is tied to your iTunes account. When you backup, or sync, your iPad in iTunes, any purchases made in iTunes or in the iPad's App Store are then recorded and your account is updated. The added advantage is that your iPad is updated and copies of the apps and other data such as documents are stored on your iTunes computer.

Important: This means that if you get a paid app during a promotion that allows you to get it for free, you will still be able to update any future versions even after the promotion ends. I know of a number of people who monitor apps and when they have a promotion giving the app for free, they will install the app even if they don't need it right at that moment. If you want to do this, my recommendation is to purchase the apps from iTunes on your computer and then move them to your iPad as needed. Basically, you are turning iTunes into an app library.

App Terminology

Software developers are usually in the business of selling software or selling advertisements. One of the big issues with mobile apps is that most of the apps themselves are not very expensive. This can be a double-edged sword - since they don't cost very much, the developer can't really do a lot of marketing or customer cultivation, so the apps almost have to sell themselves or the developer has to sell a lot of advertisement in order to make the app to pay for itself, much less make money for the developer. In fact, only a very few of the 121,000 developers even break even. Yes, you hear wonderful stories, but most - in the 90%+ range - lose money. Keep that in mind the next time you buy an app.

There are a couple of terms for searching apps that can help you make better buying decisions.

Free and LITE versions:

Some software is just free, in fact there is a ton of free software that is full-featured and very usable. Simply put, this is a great thing. Experiment and you will find all sorts of usable software.

Sometimes you will come across two versions of the same software. One may be called "Lite" or the other may be called "Pro" or "Full."

The Lite version is usually, but not always, a full version of the software with some of the software turned off. For example, it may be a spelling game and you get a sample of words instead of the whole library. The advantage of these versions is that you can really use the app and understand how well it is going to work for you before you spend any money to get the full version. I highly recommend downloading and installing a Lite version to try yourself and even with your user before you buy a full version. Just make sure that once you buy the full version you remove the Lite version from the iPad. I have had issues with my son finding the Lite version and thinking it was broken and getting frustrated.

Sometimes this same concept is used within an app title, but they use the word "Pro" in the title to signify that the Pro version is the full version. I have also seen the Pro title used to signify that it contains no advertising while the other version does, even though both versions are full-featured. Depending on a number of factors, you may prefer to not have any advertising at all, so by all means, pay for the apps.

 Note: Free apps may use advertising to pay for themselves. Some app developers use advertising to pay for app development. In principle, I am ok with this. You want to make sure the advertising is not inappropriate for your user. You also want to turn off in-app purchases. You may even want to turn off the internet browser to prevent a user from following links in the apps to websites. In all the instances I have seen, these links have just been to the developer's website to buy more apps from them. For me, though, I want my users to focus on the app and not on buying new ones.

Pro or Plus Version:

"Pro" or "Plus" is often used to reference the version of the app that you pay for, in comparison to a lite or free version. Some developers produce the exact same app in two versions, one with advertising, the other without. The Pro or Plus version is usually the one without advertising. In some apps, the pro or plus versions also have added features. Each set of apps and app developers is different.

HD Version:

The Apple iOS operating system was originally designed for the smaller format iPhone and iPod Touch, so for the 3 years before the iPad came out, there was only one size app. When the iPad was released, it had a much larger screen, which meant that developers could put more on each page. The developers had to decide how to address the change in screen size. Some developers created a second HD, or high definition, version of their apps; other developers did not.

For example, you can have an app that is both an iPhone app and an iPad app and the only difference between them is that the iPad version's title has an "HD" in it to signify the larger format. If you only have one device and it is an iPad, then always go with the HD version even if the apps are identical. The graphics will look better when they are designed for the larger format. There are apps that are only available in HD, so they can only be used with the iPad. On the other hand, if you have both an iPhone/iPod Touch and an iPad, and the app will be used on both devices AND you don't want to buy both versions of the app, consider buying the smaller version and using it on both sized devices.

The work around for any smaller app used on the iPad is that the iPad has a feature that can enlarge the smaller screen view to the size of the larger iPad screen. The graphics are not as sharp, but the application is certainly usable. The way the feature works is that when the app launches as a smaller format app, the operating system adds a small button in the lower right hand corner of the screen with a 1x or 2x on it. When the screen is in smaller scale, you will see a 2x button. When you touch it, it will enlarge the screen and then you will see the button change to 1x. Touching the 1x will reverse the process.

 Tip: I have seen it with my own child and with others, they can obsess on enlarging and reducing the size of the screen; it becomes a game. There is no way to turn off the feature. The good news is that most kids get tired of it. It can also be hit accidentally. What I have observed is that most fascinations with the button pass and most kids learn to not touch it accidentally.

Searching on a Separate Computer: iTunes

One of the ways to find apps is to use a computer and the iTunes Store. There are a number of advantages to this method:

1. You can use a keyword to do all of your searching
2. When you select an app, download it, then sync it with your iPad, it is effectively backed-up
3. You can search apps and podcasts, iTunes U and books (i.e., a number of informational sources) in one search. This is helpful when you are looking for informational content.

Disadvantage:

1. You have to sync the app with the iPad before you can use it

To search in iTunes:

1. Launch iTunes on your computer
2. Click on iTunes Store in library (this will limit the search box in the next step to just searching within the iTunes library and not your personal library on the computer)

3. In search window, search for app
4. Click results either under the heading of iPhone Apps or iPad Apps
5. Review the apps it finds

Screenshot of iTunes Search Results for "Spelling"

To give you a couple of examples of consolidating information, I ran these two search terms with the following results:

"Fine motor" Results:[*]

Result Category	Result Count
iPhone apps	8 total apps
iPad apps	8 total apps, 3 are common with iPhone apps
Podcasts	16
Books:	2
Albums	17
iTunes U	3

"Drag and release" Results*

Result Category	Result Count
iPhone apps	2 total apps
Podcasts	5

* I find it very interesting that when you do the same searches in the iTunes Store via the computer and on the App Store via iPad that you get different results. I did the same two searches within minutes of each other and in both cases the App Store yielded more results.

Searching Via iPad

You can search for apps in the App Store on the iPad. There are, of course, pros and cons to doing searches this way.

Advantages:

1. Once downloaded, you can immediately use the app

Disadvantages:

1. You will have to sync to back up later
2. If you are doing a lot of searching, a physical keyboard can be more comfortable to use than the iPad virtual keyboard

To search for apps via the App Store:

Tap on the App Store icon
Tap in the search bar in the upper right hand corner
Enter your search terms
Tap on the Search button on the keypad to launch your search

Screenshot Searching Results App Store for "Spelling"

Searching using the App Store

"Fine Motor" Search Results:*

Result Category	Result Count
iPhone apps	12
iPad Apps	11

"Drag and Release" Search Results:*

Result Category	Result Count
iPhone apps	5
iPad Apps	2

* I find it very interesting that when you do the same searches in the iTunes Store via the computer and on the App Store via iPad that you get different results. I did the same two searches within minutes of each other and in both cases the App Store

yielded more results.

Example Filters and Searches in the App Store

You can also filter the search results in the App Store using certain criteria:

1. **Category** - These are all of the App Store/iTunes major categories of apps. I have not found it to be particularly useful for finding good apps for special needs using category alone. I may use it to get a quick look-see, but if you were to look at all of the apps on Noah's iPad you would see many different categories, including medical, games, education, and productivity.
2. **Release Date** - This is date the app was released. I will look at the date it was released very carefully and specifically at the last updated date. It can be found on the app page itself under the category in the left hand column under the app icon. Between this date and any version number, it will let me know if the app is still growing and being loved.
3. **Customer Rating** - Overall average rating for the app made by customers. While I use this info to get a general sense of how well an app may function, I do not use it as an automatic filter for apps.
4. **Price** - The cost of the App. This is a good filter for a broad overview or for quick searches.
5. **Device** - This will let you if it is for iPhone only or for larger devices. You will have dig deeper into the app to find out if the app was really make for the iPad or just made for the iPhone but has a 2x button to enlarge the screen.

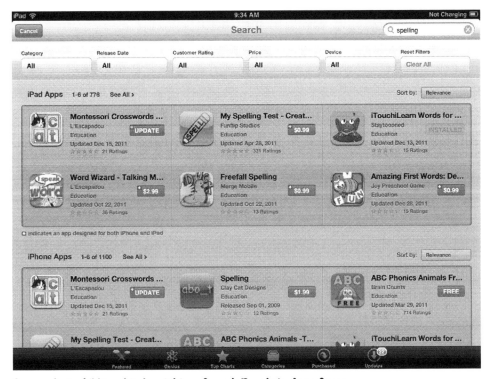

Screenshot of Filter Totals within a Search Result in Apps Store

Other Ways to Find Apps

There are many ways to find apps outside of iTunes and the App Store. Here are ones that I use and think you should keep in mind.

Searching Via Computer: Internet

Searching the internet directly for apps can be a hit or miss proposition.

Advantages:

1. You have more content to search. This can be a hit.
2. Apps can be referenced by both the developer and other users like you
3. There are a number of great resources to help you with Apps, specifically for special needs and with other general topics - for example, education
4. There are better search tools than just keywords used in iTunes or App Store

Disadvantages:

- You have more content to search. This can be a miss and when you miss on the internet, it can be a big time-waster

- There are many websites to sort out, perspectives to consider

Recommendations for Searching the Internet for Apps:

1. Follow blogs to find apps: There are many blogs relating to many different special needs areas on the internet. Find out what apps the bloggers you follow like and use their blogs to read about them.
2. Follow Developers websites: If you find an app developer you like, follow them. It is likely they will create more apps you like and that work for you.
3. Search for skill development to find blogs and articles about how to develop the skills your user needs. Understand how they develop those skills and then use that to search for apps.

BridgingApps.org

Of course I am going to plug the website I help to create and build. That is why I helped to create and build it - to help people, you in fact, use the iPad and other technology like it to have an impact on your loved ones with special needs. BridgingApps.org (formerly SNApps4kids.com) can help in a number of ways, but I want to highlight two in particular:

Insignio Search: *http://www.bridgingapps.org/screen/* We built a custom search that looks at three websites. Apple iTunes, Android Market and Bridgingapps.org and searches all three sites using custom search technology. The advantage of search technology is that it is more than just keyword searching - it tries to take your search string and bring more pertinent results than you would get with just keyword alone. It delivers more desirable results. Plus it is only searching three sites and not the whole internet.

BridgingApps App Reviews: We developed a skills-based app review system that catalogs apps in ways more meaningful to special needs users than just a broad category like education or games. All of the reviews are done by an occupational therapist, speech therapist, or special education teacher. And as a part of the review, each app is used with a special needs user.

App Finder Apps

So this is funny. There are apps that help you find apps. There are many of them out there so I am just going to highlight one of them, but I would look around. Each app - and usually the accompanying website - has its own way of organizing apps, searching and its own method of suggesting apps, so you will have try a few to find the ones you like. They make money by selling you apps, so keep this in mind when you look at their suggestions. One of the effective ways I have seen these apps be used is to monitor for apps doing a free promotion, so you can grab a paid app for free during the promotional period. When it goes back to being a paid for app, you still have the full version, upgrades and all.

App Hits for iPad

Cost: Free
Developer: Sane Apps LLC
iTunes URL: *http://itunes.apple.com/us/app/app-hits-for-ipad-discover/id417716440?mt=8*

With App Hits for iPad you can quickly see the stack ranking of apps, if they go on sale, and by how much the price has dropped. It looks at both free and paid apps. It

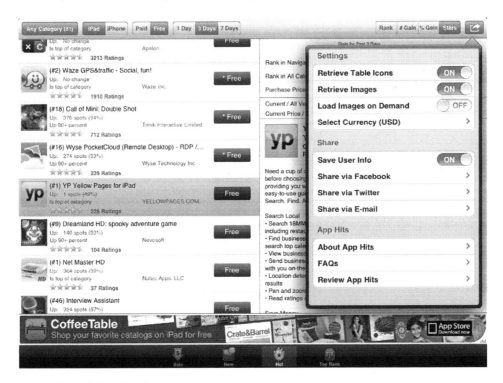

Screenshot of App Hits App

only tracks the top 400 in each category, though, so it is not the entire iTunes library. A lot of good apps will not be in the list, just the popular ones.

App Store Genius Recommendations Feature

One of the App Store features I use quite a bit is the Genius Recommendations. You have to turn the feature on in order to use it. It looks at other apps that you have bought and makes recommendations based upon those apps. You can narrow the categories in which it provides recommendations by selecting a category and seeing the results. The results will get better and more numerous as you buy and download more apps (free and paid). I have found a number of very interesting apps this way. You will still have to do your own research on the apps, but it is a very nice starting point.

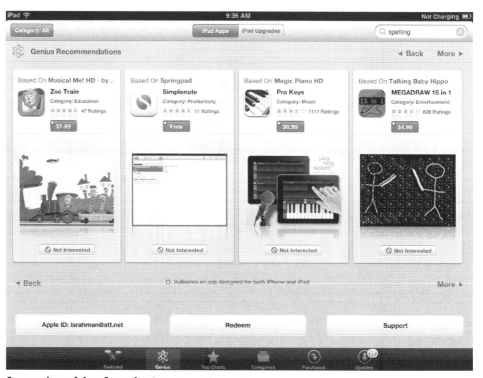

Screenshot of App Store Genius suggestion screen

Web Resources for Finding Special Needs Apps

There are a lot of web resources for finding apps. Some of the resources sponsored by major non-profit organizations:

1. BridgingApps.org, sponsored by Easter Seals of Greater Houston (formerly SNApps4kids.com): Website: *http://www.bridgingapps.org*
2. The National Association of Child Development, Website: http://www.nacd.org NACD's Application Blog: *http://apps.nacd.org*
3. Ohio Center for Autism and Low Incidence Disabilities (OCALI), Website *http://ocali.org*
4. IEAR.org Education Apps Review, Website: *http://www.iear.org*

There are also a number of great private blogs run by parents, teachers and therapists, too many to list here. Plus, the list changes constantly, but do a quick internet search and you will find an ample selection. Here is the criteria I use to determine the perspective of the blogs and websites that review special needs apps:

1. Who is the primary person(s) behind the website? Are they parents, are they educators, are they therapists?
2. What perspective do they have? Professional? Are they talking from the perspective of a disability that is the same or similar to the ones I focus on?
3. Why are they providing this information? For educational purposes, for profit, for catharsis?
4. What is the information on the website or blog focused on? App review, training, special needs, general?
5. What advertising is on the website, if any? What kind?
6. Are there product reviews? Do they disclose if the products/apps are provided for free?

In general, like all information on the web, take the good stuff and leave behind the stuff that isn't useful.

General Comment About Buying Apps

Some general tips for buying apps:

Look for apps that are loved: This can mean apps that customers love or that developers love.

1. Customer Love: Read through the comments, look at the star ratings, what are customers saying about the app? Make sure you skip over the marketing comments - if they look too good to be true, they aren't, they are paid for.
2. Developer Love: There are big developers and small developers. Most are

small. They develop not because they are making any real money, they most often develop something they think the world needs or think will be valuable to someone else. Here is how you know if the developer loves their app.

- Read the description: You can tell by how they talk about it if they are proud of what they have done.

- Look at the release date: Has the app been around a while?

- Look at the version number: Has it been updated at all? A lot? Not at all? Either side of the spectrum maybe a bad thing. No updates suggest no love. Too many updates may mean lots of bugs or lack of direction.

- Look at their other apps: This will give you sense of how big they are.

- Go to their website: Find out if they are focused on getting customer feedback, how big they are, what they are about.

3. Keep in Mind:

- The number of comments or lack thereof is not necessarily a sign of love. There are some apps that won't have a lot of comments simply because they don't appeal to a large audience. We have a number of medical apps that just don't get downloaded or commented on much, but they are great apps.

- People can pay for comments, and soft advertising appears in the comment section, so don't believe everything you read. Experiment yourself.

- Most apps are repurposed for a special needs user, so your goals and the developer's goals are not likely to be exactly the same. Some things will work, others will not. Don't be afraid to experiment to determine what works best for you.

- Special needs apps are good because they were developed for the special needs community. That does not mean that they were developed exactly for your user. It does mean that the developer is usually very open to hearing your feedback, so contact them if you have an issue, comment, or feedback.

Tip: App tips, tricks and considerations:

1. Test a Lite version of the app first if you not sure of it.
2. Clean unused apps and Lite versions after you have installed the full version
3. Rotate your apps just like you would toys
4. Keep an eye out for paid apps that become free for a limited time. If you can get them when they are free, you will always have them, even when they become paid. All updates are free for the life of the app.

Testing and Removing Apps

This section will cover testing and removing apps. Included are

5. What to look for when testing
1. Testing Tips and Tricks
2. How to remove apps
3. When to remove apps

Testing Apps

Here are the questions I ask when I test an app:

1. Content:

   - Is this content suitable for my users?

   - Are they going to like it? Relate to it?

   - Am I going to be able to deal with hearing it over and over again?

2. Skills:

   - What skills does it help support?

   - Can I get these skills supported in another app I already own? This answer may be yes and I might still get the app. In therapy, you often have to do the same things over and over again. Putting a different face on it can help.

- Are the skills and level of function appropriate?

- Are my user's skills and level of function appropriate?

3. Usability:

- Do I understand how it works?

- Is it easy enough for my users? Or too easy?

- Does it work?

4. Marketing, Advertising, Links:

- Does it have too much advertising? I have seen apps that put so much advertising in the startup screen I can't even find the start button.

- Is there advertising? If so, it is appropriate?

- Are there links to other sites? Are they appropriate?

- Is the content I want front and center?

5. App Settings

- Is the setting button in the app, in settings, or both?

- What can I control?

- What can I start with and how far can they grow into the app?

6. Lite Versions and In-app Purchases:

- How much of the app do I get? Is the content complete?

- How many upgrades (in app purchases) do I need to make to make the app complete? I have seen free apps cost as much as $50 to upgrade and get all of the content.

- Is the upgraded content worth it?

- Is there a way either inside the app or via the iPad settings that I can control buying and prevent the user from getting side-tracked and frustrated?

7. Other things:

- Is this a known developer? Do I like their other work?

- What do I know about the app, uses, reviews, or recommendations?

8. Cost:

- What is the cost of the app now?

- What is the cost for additional content?

I know this is a long list, but not everything will apply to every app and you will start to get a sense of the buying process, so the time it takes you will shorten dramatically.

Removing Apps

I regularly remove apps from my iPads. There are a ton of reasons to do it, so you need to know how.

Apps can be removed 2 ways:

1. On the iPad
2. Via iTunes

Removing Apps Via the iPad

Removing Apps directly from the iPad:

1. Scroll to the page and find the app you want to remove
2. Touch and hold the icon for a few seconds until the icon starts to jiggle
3. Remove your finger
4. The icon will now have a small X in the upper left hand cover. To remove the app, tap on the X. The app will disappear.

Note: If you touch and hold an icon and it does not jiggle after a second or two, then you likely have the Delete App setting turned off. Go to **Settings**, **General, Restrictions** and turn it back on, then try again.

Note: The next time you sync with iTunes, the app will reappear unless you deselect the app in iTunes on the App page of the iPad. Go to iTunes, select your iPad, go to the App page and deselect the app.

Screenshot of Deleting App on iPad

Removing Apps Via iTunes

1. Connect the iPad to your computer
2. Launch iTunes if it does not do so automatically
3. Select your iPad
4. Select the App page. You will see a list of Apps.
5. Deselect the app you want to remove
6. Apply Changes
7. On the Summary page press **Sync** to sync the iPad with iTunes. This will re-move the app from the iPad

Screenshot of App Deselected in iTunes

Screenshot of App Selected in iTunes

Creating Your Own Content

There may be times when you may not find what you are looking for, or know that if you could create your own content, it would be better. Here are a few ways I have created my own content or have seen other people do it.

When creating content, there are going to be a couple of things you want to keep in mind. First, think about what action and what response you want to create. For example, if you want to create a simple choice board, you might want to keep the action and response very simple, and have a group of photos in the Photo library from which to choose. However, if you want to create a book with pages and you want each page to flip forward (but not backward) and you want to add audio to each page, you might use a flashcard program like Flashcard Creator or even a book creation app. On the other hand, if you want to create a simple choice among 3 items, you might use Powerpoint or Keynote®. If instead you want total control, you may want to create your own software. The point is that you need to think through the actions and responses you want to create then pick the method you feel is the best and easiest way to create and deliver that experience. There is likely a way to create what you need using readily available tools.

Photos

You can create simple story boards and/or choice boards just by organizing your photos in the Photo program. What you will need to do

1. You will need photos either previously taken, items from the internet, or photos taken on the iPad 2.
2. If you have photos on another device, they need to be available to you on your iPad

   - Sync the photos on your computer to your iPad using iTunes. In doing so, you can also move them over in the folder structure you would like to have on the iPad.

   - Use iCloud or Dropbox.

   - Use Apple iPad Camera Connection Kit. This USB adapter plugs into the 30 pin port and will allow you to either connect your camera to the iPad and download pictures or connect the memory card to the iPad to download them

   - Download them from your website, FaceBook, etc and save them to your iPad's Photo library

Note: When using Photos as a choice board system, the icons of the photos are small. There are 35 icons per page. Once you select a photo, it will enlarge to full screen. For someone with fine motor control issues, this may be too many icons per page and there is no way to control the number. You may want to use a choice board program like My Choice Board instead (see Chapter 8 regarding AAC for more details).

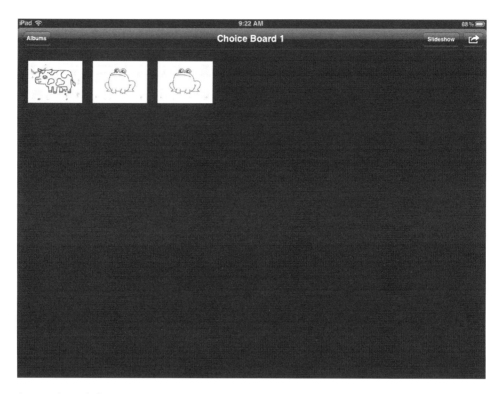

Screenshot of iPhoto Album as Choice Board

Organizing Photos on the iPad

To organize photos in the Photo app on the iPad, follow these steps:

1. Tap the **Photo** app icon and navigate to the **Albums** area of Photo. It is likely you will be in a photo area and not the albums area, if so tap on the **Albums** arrow in the upper left hand corner.
2. In **Albums**, tap the **Edit** button in the upper right hand corner.
3. In Albums edit mode, tap the **New Album** button in the upper left hand corner
4. Enter a name for your new album, some thing like Choice Board 1, tap **Save.**
5. You will automatically be presented with all of the photos in the entire photo library and asked to choose which photos you want in the new album. Tap to select a photo, tap again to deselect a photo. Tap **Done,** in the upper right hand corner when done. You now have a new album.

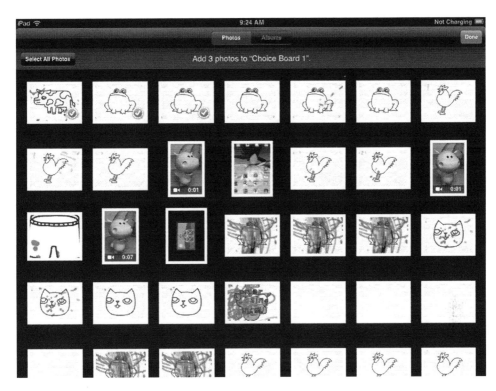

Screenshot of Adding Photos to album in iPhoto app

 Note: The organizational feature of iPhoto is available on iOS versions 5.0 and above. If you are not running iOS 5.0 or above, see alternatives to iPhoto below.

Photo-Sort for iPad
Cost:$2
Developer: Romain HENRY
iTunes URL: *http://itunes.apple.com/us/app/photo-sort-for-ipad-organize/ id369610590?mt=8*

This program is an alternative to Apple Photo and allows you to sort photos and create folders on the iPad without needing an external computer and iTunes. In other words, it allows you to perform this function on the go.

Screenshot of Photo-Sort for iPad

Flashcards

There are a number of flashcard programs in the App Store. You can create your own content by importing photos and recording your own audio. The advantage of creating your own flashcards is that you can have text and record audio specifically to go with each flashcard. The flashcards can be used for learning or communication and can be customized to be exactly what you want and need.

Screenshot of Sample Flashcard

Picture Card Maker (Free and Plus)

Cost: Free, Plus version $6
Developer: Bo Innovations
iTunes URL: *http://itunes.apple.com/us/app/picture-card-maker-for-communication/*
id419089000?mt=8

Picture Card Maker and Picture Card Maker Plus are both flashcard creation
programs. The Plus version does not contain any advertising and gives you many
different picture card options, like custom sized cards, text control, and edit control to
prevent card deletion, to name a few. To create a card, you can take a picture or use
a picture already in your library, you then can add an audio clip, recorded directly on
the iPad, and text for the card.

Screensho of Picture Card Make

Powerpoint and Keynote

Microsoft Powerpoint and Apple Keynote both are presentation creation and delivery software for your desktop or laptop computer. You can create content on the computer using all of the powerful features and the ease of using a computer, and then use the iPad to present them. I have used this to create simple books in Arabic for Noah. With Powerpoint and Keynote, you can create buttons or objects that take you from one page to another when pushed, as well as swipe forward and backwards. These buttons can be used for more than just navigation; they can also be used to create a level of interactivity close to creating your own programs. In fact, using presentation is how a lot of software developers mockup applications for the iPad. You will need an app to play the presentations on the iPad. I have used and recommend Keynote, but there are a number of presentation players for the iPad.

 Note: Keynote on the iPad will play both Keynote and Powerpoint presentations, but does not play audio stored inside the presentation.

Note: Not all animations and functions of the full desktop/laptop version of the presentation playback software work on Keynote for the iPad.

Keynote

Cost: $10
Developer: Apple
iTunes URL: *http://itunes.apple.com/us/app/keynote/id361285480?mt=8*

This application will allow you to play Powerpoint or play and create Keynote presentations directly on the iPad. The app is very easy to use, but some users may need help launching presentations.
App Icon

Screenshot of Keynote

Movies

Video can make for a very controlled way to deliver content to the iPad. My dad took a children's book he had of the Arabic alphabet and scanned each page into the computer. Using iMovie® on the Mac®, he brought each scan into iMovie as a picture and then did a voice over reading each letter and the caption underneath. He then exported it into a movie format that was then imported into the iPad. My son loves hearing my dad's voice on the video.

With that success, he then used the title program in iMovie to do the numbers in Arabic from 1 to 20 and used his voice to count them. One of the things he realized even before we added them to Noah's iPad was that with video you only have one speed, so he ended up doing a few versions at different speeds. This is an important point for educational content. As you learn, the speed at which you can receive information changes. Video only has one speed, so it is something you need to think about when creating content.

Another downside to video is the size of each of the files. If you have a lot of video you can fill up an iPad pretty quickly, so keep an eye out and rotate your content. That said, for customized content, video is a great method of creation and delivery.

 ### A Story Before Bed
Cost: subscription service $40 (25 books), $70 (50 books) and $100 (250 books) per year.
Developer: http://www.astorybeforebed.com/
iTunes URL: *http://itunes.apple.com/us/app/a-story-before-bed-personalized/id364887654?mt=8*

This is a different aspect to the video idea. Using a computer, you, a grandparent, caregiver, or anyone else you like can record themselves reading a story that the user can later play back, hearing the story with your voice and seeing a video of you at the same time. Turn the page in either direction and it will skip the video and audio to that point in the book.

Advantage:

• Anyone with your login and an internet connection can record a book for your child or user, across the street or across the country.

Disadvantage:

- It has to be one of their books and cannot be your own content. That said, it seems like a great way to personalize the reading experience.

Screenshot of A Story Before Bed

iMovie
Cost: $5
Developer: Apple
iTunes URL: *http://itunes.apple.com/us/app/imovie/id377298193?mt=8*

iMovie is an app that allows you to edit and produce video directly on your iPad. While not as feature rich as iMovie on the Mac, it does allow you to create full video that can be played back on the iPad. A word of caution, video takes up a lot of space, so if you are going to create it on the iPad, you will want to manage and remove all used video after you have created your finished product.

Screenshot of iMovie

Explain Everything

Cost: $3
Developer: MorrisCooke
iTunes URL: *http://itunes.apple.com/us/app/explain-everything/id431493086?mt=8*

This app lets you have multiple pages of screenshots within a project. You can then draw on them and record your voice to create anything from training videos to demos to homework assignments. Explain Everything not only lets you export and share in a number of ways, it also lets you export and share your project files and not just the finished project. This includes the ability to save to Dropbox. This is a great feature.

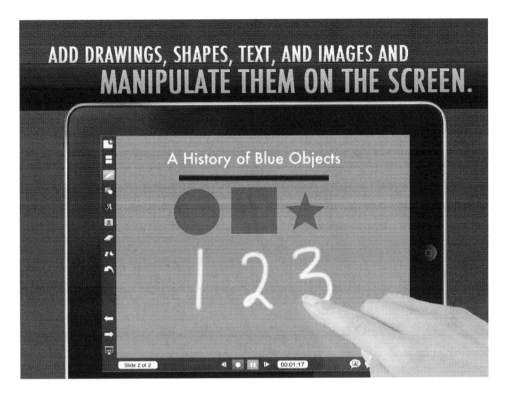

Screenshot of Explain Everything

Create Your Own Books

Using programs like the StoryBuddy app, you can create your own books for your kids. This can be incredibly rewarding and can allow you target and create the exact content you are seeking. It can also be very time consuming, so plan well. Make sure you have good goals and I recommend starting small, experimenting with your user and seeing if it is a workable medium for both of you.

StoryBuddy

Cost: $8
Developer: Tapfuze
iTunes URL: *http://itunes.apple.com/us/app/storybuddy/id390538762?mt=8*

StoryBuddy allows you to quickly and easily create simple story books for your users. The program allows you to create and present multiple books. It has a very simple navigation system for your user and a clear and easy creation system for you. You can import your own pictures. It does not allow you add your own audio. You can, however, export or email your creation to others.

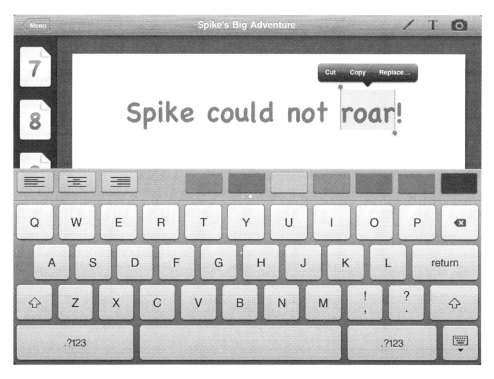

Screenshot of StoryBuddy

Create Your Own Lessons

There are a number of applications designed to create and deliver interactive lessons and learning to both computers and the iPad. Since this book is focused on special needs, I want to highlight a company that has been bringing interactive creation and delivery tools designed specifically for the special needs market. The company is Monarch Teaching Technologies Inc., and the product is Vizzle. Vizzle was developed as a way to create, share and deliver interactive learning for children and young adults with autism by way of touchboard, touch and table computers. It now has an iPad player as well.

What I like about the system is that there is a whole online library of content created for the Vizzle community by teachers and other professionals for special needs users that you can freely access and use. In fact, all of the lessons are created online (public or private) and then delivered through a number of different devices. The program is licensed by how many people create material, not by how many users use each lesson. Vizzle does not post official pricing on their website, it is done on a per case basis, but for my son's teacher it was about $700 for the year. Parents have a different rate. This is expensive for one user, but for a classroom this is a bargain. They literally use the software every day to create all sorts of interactive material for their smart board and iPads and it has dramatically changed the classroom.

Vizzle Player

Cost: Free (Author is by subscription)
Developer: Monarch Teaching Technologies, Inc.
iTunes URL: *http://itunes.apple.com/us/app/vizzle-player/id474594699?mt=8*

Vizzle Player allows you to playback interactive content created on the Vizzle Platform

Screenshot of Vizzle Player

Create Your Own Software

It may seem like a lot of work to create your own app, but a lot of the first special needs apps were created by parents and other caregivers who saw a need and went about filling it. Some of them became developers, while some of them found people to develop for them. If you see a need and are so inclined, you may want to consider developing software of your own. For those who are not full developers but are technically inclined, there is application builder software for iOS. Buzztouch, for example, allows you build applications visually for free and then allows you export the source code used in Apple development tools to compile the software.

 Note: All software available in the iTunes store must first be reviewed and approved by Apple.

Buzztouch

Cost: Free
Developer:
iTunes URL: *http://www.buzztouch.com*

Application development software that allows non-developers to create and build their own iOS software. This software allows you to visually build and test your own application. When the app is ready, it exports the source code to your computer and using the iOS development tools, you make an executable version of the software (compile). You can then send the app to Apple and get it approved for installation on your or other people's systems.

Button Crazy: Things You Should Know About iPad Buttons

In this section we will cover the combinations, navigation, tips and tricks you can use with the different iPad buttons. There are a lot of options, some you will want to use with your user, others for yourself.

The Home Button Explained

The Home Button is the most powerful of the all of the buttons on the iPad. Below is a table to explain its many uses:

Home Button Combinations	Where Am I When I Do This?	What Happens Next?	Notes
Single Tap on Home Button	iPad is Off	Nothing happens	

Home Button Combinations	Where Am I When I Do This?	What Happens Next?	Notes
Single Tap on Home Button	IPad is in Standby Mode	Turns on iPad lock screen, slide to unlock	
Single Tap on Home Button	First Page of Home Screen	Slide to Search Screen	
Single Tap on Home Button	Any other page of Home Screen	Slide to First Page of Home Screen	
Single Tap on Home Button	Search Page	Slide to First Page of Home Screen	
Single Tap on Home Button	In an App	Go to Home Page	
Double Tap on Home Button	IPad is Off	Nothing happens	
Double Tap on Home Button	IPad is in Standby Mode	Turns on iPad lock screen and displays audio controls, slide to unlock	
Double Tap on Home Button	First Page of Home Screen	Displays Multitasking User Interface at bottom of screen	
Double Tap on Home Button	Any other page of Home Screen	Displays Multitasking User Interface at bottom of screen	
Double Tap on Home Button	Search Page	Displays Multitasking User Interface at bottom of screen	
Double Tap on Home Button	In an App	Displays Multitasking User Interface at bottom of screen	
Triple Tap on Home Button	IPad is Off	Nothing happens	

Home Button Combinations	Where Am I When I Do This?	What Happens Next?	Notes
Triple Tap on Home Button	IPad is in Standby Mode	Nothing happens unless VoiceOver is selected as default function for Triple Home Button press; if so, it will toggle between On and Off	
Triple Tap on Home Button	First Page of Home Screen	Launches Accessibility Feature determined in Settings program	Choose from: Off, VoiceOver, White on Black, Zoom, AssistiveTouch, Ask (will ask you which of the 4 options you would like)
Triple Tap on Home Button	Any other page of Home Screen	Launches Accessibility Feature determined in Settings program	Choose from: Off, VoiceOver, White on Black, Zoom, AssistiveTouch, Ask (will ask you which of the 4 options you would like)
Triple Tap on Home Button	Search Page	Launches Accessibility Feature determined in Settings program	Choose from: Off, VoiceOver, White on Black, Zoom, AssistiveTouch, Ask (will ask you which of the 4 options you would like)
Triple Tap on Home Button	In an App	Launches Accessibility Feature determined in Settings program	Choose from: Off, VoiceOver, White on Black, Zoom, AssistiveTouch, Ask (will ask you which of the 4 options you would like)

How to Take a Screenshot

To take a screenshot on the iPad:

1. To take a screenshot of the exact screen you are currently seeing, tap and hold the Home Button
2. While still holding the Home Button, tap the Power Button once.
3. The screen will flash white for a split second and if your speaker is not muted, you will hear a camera shutter sound.
4. You will find your screenshot in the Photos library on the iPad
5. You can use the share button in Photo to send it via email, etc. or use sync to move it to a computer.

Use iPhoto to Download and Organize Photos from the iPad

 Tip: While making this book I took a lot of screenshots. Instead of using the share button to move each one off the iPad, I used iPhoto. After completing a series of screenshots, I plugged my iPad into my laptop, a Mac running iPhoto. Because this was not the same computer I use to sync my iPad, it would launch iTunes and iPhoto at the same time and ask me if I wanted to move my account to this iTunes. I would always cancel, but in iPhoto I would see all of the Albums on the iPad. I would then select the photos I wanted and import them into iPhoto.

MultiTasking Gestures

Multitasking Gestures are a new feature on the iPad as of iOS 5. They are designed to help navigate the iPad using gestures instead of buttons and provide a short cut to navigate around the iPad. They are turned off by default, but once they are turned on, from any location on the iPad, you can:

1. Navigate to and from the Home Screen: Four or Five finger Pinch
2. Open the Multitasking User Interface: Four or Five finger swipe upwards
3. Switch to a previously used app: Four or Five finger swipe to the left.

   - Keep swiping, you will keep going backward in order of the apps used

   - Swipe to the right at any time, and move forward in the apps used.

 Note: This feature can work against a user who has fine motor control issues. If the feature is turned on and someone accidentally swipes with their whole hand, it could create an unwelcome and possibly confusing action. So use this feature with caution.

How to Turn on Multitasking Gestures

To Turn on Multitasking Gestures, within **Settings** tap **General,** and tap on **Multitasking Gestures** to turn on or off.

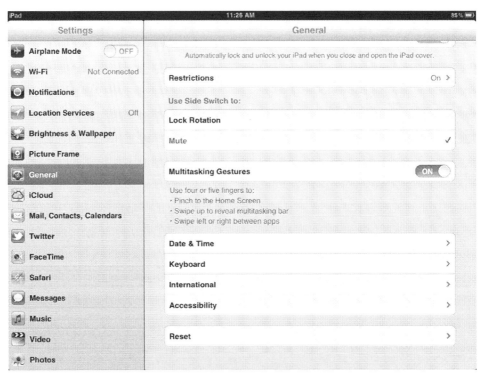

Screenshot of Multitasking Gestures Turn On

Mute Button vs Screen Rotation

The slider on the right hand side of the iPad above the volume rocker is programable with two options. The default option is to Mute and Unmute the iPad. You can instead choose to have it Lock or Unlock the screen rotation function. If you have a user who is just starting out and fine/gross motor control is an issue, or if the user gets confused by the screen flipping around a lot, I would recommend setting the slider to control screen rotation lock. If, on the other hand, you have a user who loves everything at extreme volumes, then you may want to keep the default mute/unmute setting. Think about it in terms of what you may need to control quickly on the device.

How to Set the Slider Option

To change the default action of the slider:

1. In **Settings**, **General** under the section **Use Side Switch to**, choose either

    • Default, which is mute; or

    • Tap on **Lock Rotation** to change

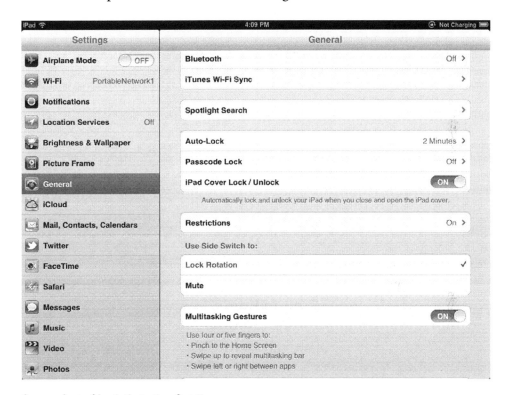

Screenshot of Lock Rotation Setting

CHAPTER

10

Maintenance & Trouble-shooting

In this chapter we will cover:

1. Backup
2. Maintenance
3. Troubleshooting

Backup Maintenance

It is important that you backup your iPad on a regular basis. There are two separate commands that will cause a backup - by pressing the backup command in iTunes, or by syncing. Both will backup the device. Backups are especially important if you are using any sort of media (for example, pictures or video) for communication or scheduling, or if you are using any sort of AAC, flashcard, word processor or book software where you create a lot of custom content directly on the iPad. Here is the horror story. You spend hours, weeks building custom communication boards and something really bad happens to the iPad. If you haven't done a backup/sync, it is now all gone. Further, you are regularly going to change your schedules or communication boards, so if you don't continue to backup, you are putting yourself at high risk.

Let's step back and explain what is actually on the iPad and what is being backed up. The iPad has the following types of data:

1. Operating System: this data is not backed up during the backup process. It is about 2GB worth of data.
2. Applications (Apps): the record of each application purchased (free or for pay) is backed up every time you do a backup. The applications themselves are not backed up, as Apple has a copy of all of them on their servers.
3. Media and Documents: this could be music from iTunes or photos, video, email, presentations, or documents created on another device and moved to the iPad or created directly on the iPad. If the data is not anywhere else and you use it a lot - think video scheduling, video modeling, books and stories you have created for and with your users, anything created on the iPad - it is important information and needs to be backed up.
4. AAC, Video Modeling, Video Scheduling and any other highly important, frequently used data. While this is technically a subset of Media and Documents, I want to highlight how crucial this data can be to backup. If the iPad is a primary communication device and you don't back it up, you are putting your whole strategy at a high risk of failure. You could be changing pages daily while using an AAC application, and you would not want to lose any of that.

 Note: For more information on setting up Sync, see chapter 4, Syncing, for a more in-depth discussion.

The Difference Between Sync and Backup

There is a difference between syncing and backing up an iPad:

1. Backup. This is a command found in iTunes when you right click on the iPad name. This function makes a copy of what is currently on your iPad
2. Sync. This can be done either via iTunes, wired or wireless, or via iCloud. It also makes a copy of what's on your iPad, but also adds any new data from iTunes or iCloud to your iPad.

Should I Backup or Sync?

You will likely use Sync to backup your iPad more than you will use backup alone.

Pros of using Sync:

1. Bidirectional. Information, media, etc. moves from the computer to the iPad
2. Backup and data sync are done using one command. You only need to keep up 1 good habit.
3. Sync can be done wirelessly via wi-fi or via iCloud
4. Sync can be done automatically via wi-fi or via iCloud

Cons of Sync:

1. You may only need to backup and not need to sync. Think in terms of groups of users like schools or therapy groups.
2. You cannot Sync to an iTunes account if that iPad is not registered to it. You can at least backup the apps using any iTunes account
3. You can only have one iTunes account as the primary syncing app.

How Do I Backup My iPad

To backup your iPad:

1. Plug the iPad into your computer.
2. If iTunes does not launch automatically, launch iTunes.
3. When the system recognizes your iPad ("mounts"), and you can see it in iTunes, right click your mouse on the name of the iPad you want to backup and select **Backup**.

Upgrading the Operating System

To upgrade the Operating System on the iPad:

1. Launch iTunes
2. Make sure you are logged into iTunes using the proper account
3. Plug the iPad into your PC
4. If there is an update, iTunes will inform you that an update is ready. Click **Download and Update**
5. If there are any purchases that have not been transferred over to your iTunes library, then select "Cancel" and do the transfer
6. You will then get a confirmation warning you that your update will delete all apps. The apps will be restored after the update is complete. If all purchases have been transferred properly, click **Update**.
7. You will then be informed about the new features of the update; click **Next**
8. You will have to agree to any new licensing; click **Agree**
9.   iTunes will go through a process of backing up your device, installing the new update, then restoring the apps.

A new iPad software version (5.0) is available for the iPad "Maya's iPad". Would you like to download it and update your iPad now?

iTunes will verify the software update with Apple.

☐ Do not ask me again

[Cancel]   [Download Only]   [Download and Update]

There are purchased items on the iPad "Maya's iPad" that have not been transferred to your iTunes library. You should transfer these items to your iTunes library before updating this iPad. Are you sure you want to continue?

[Cancel]   [Continue]

Updating to iOS 5.0 will delete all of the apps and media, including iTunes Store purchases, on your iPad. To preserve your content, apply this update on the computer where you sync apps, music, videos, and photos.

Updating on this computer will only preserve contacts, calendars, text messages, and other settings. Please do not interrupt the update, which may take an hour or longer to complete.

(?)   [Cancel]   [Update]

○ ○ ○   iPad Software Update

iOS 5 Software Update

This update contains over 200 new features, including the following:

- Notifications
  - Swipe from the top of any screen to view notifications in one place with Notification Center
  - New notifications appear briefly at the top of the screen
  - View notifications from lock screen
  - Slide the notification app icon to the right on the lock screen to go directly to the app
- iMessage
  - Send and receive unlimited text, photo, and video messages with other iOS 5 users
  - Track messages with delivery and read receipts
  - Group messaging and secure encryption
  - Works over cellular network and Wi-Fi*
- Newsstand
  - Automatically organizes magazine and newspaper subscriptions on Home Screen
  - Displays the cover of the latest issue
  - Background downloads of new issues
- Reminders for managing to do lists

[Save]   [Cancel]   [Next]

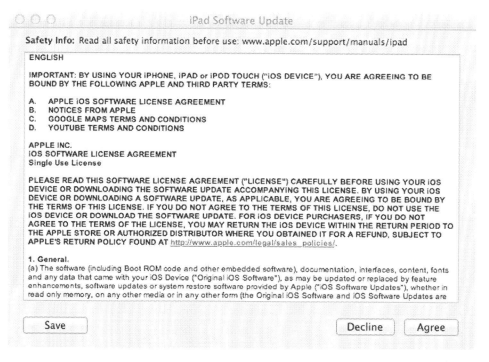

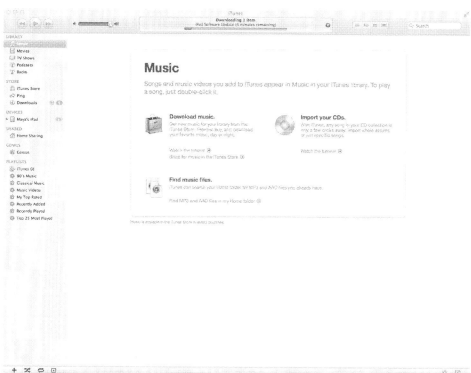

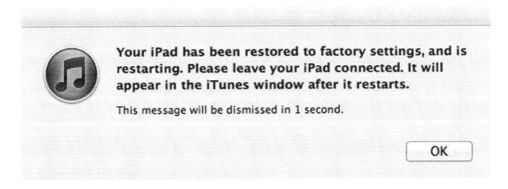

Your iPad has been restored to factory settings, and is restarting. Please leave your iPad connected. It will appear in the iTunes window after it restarts.

This message will be dismissed in 1 second.

OK

Screenshot Series of Upgrading iOS in iTunes

Tip: Always use the same iTunes library to sync your iPad. You cannot use two iTunes libraries or two computers each with their own version of iTunes even if you use the same iTunes account. If you use a second iTunes library (or a second pc) to update your iPad, for example, iTunes will ask if you want to move the primary library from the old computer to the new computer. If you complete an update on a second computer and then choose to not move the iTunes library, iTunes will NOT restore the apps during the update process and you will be left with a generic iPad.

Tip: Pick your newest and least used computer for your backups, updates and restorations. Pick a new computer because you will likely have your iPad a while, and by putting it on the newest computer you have, you can ensure that the data will be available for the longest time. Also, by selecting a relatively unused computer, you are decreasing the likelihood the computer will fall victim to computer viruses and corruption, again furthering the life span of your iTunes app backup. While this is not the end of the world, you can run into licensing issues and apps issues if you have used a number of different machines to update and backup.

I would also use the same machine to backup multiple iPads. This is just a continuation of doing what works, if you already have a good machine that is relatively unused in the house, then go with what already works.

In my house, instead of the laptops my wife and I had, I used a media PC that we had to do all of our backups and to maintain our iTunes library. My logic was that no one was using this machine to surf the web and download, so it was a very stable machine and was not likely to blowup anytime soon. I back it up regularly because it is on my home network, so that further adds to its stability.

Update Your Apps Regularly

You should make it a habit to update your apps regularly. When you write software, there are always unforeseen issues, so the developers fix them as they go along and release an update. Staying up-to-date with your apps will likely result in there being fewer bugs and you and your user having a better experience. The App Store will notify you when you have apps that need to be updated. This could be daily, weekly, or monthly. I find that doing a little at a time is a lot easier on my patience than doing it in one big chunk. While there is an "Update All" button, if you have more than 15-20 updates, it does not always work the first or second time, so I end up spending my time monitoring the downloads, and that is just not fun.

Note: Whenever you update the operating system, especially after a major update, make sure to update the apps. There are new features that always come out with new operating system updates, and app updates will often contain additions that will take advantage of the updates.

How to Update Your Apps

Screenshot of Update Tab in App Store

To update your apps:

1. Tap on **App Store**
2. Tap on the **Updates** tab
3. Tap on either

   - **Update All** in the upper right hand corner, or

   - Update each individual app by tapping on the button next to each app on the right hand side.

Using iTunes to Reorganize Your Apps

Screenshot of App Selected in iTunes

Have you ever wanted to easily organize the icons on the various pages of the Home screen? Well, you can do just that using iTunes and then syncing with the iPad. Here is how:

1. Start by syncing the iPad so that everything is up-to-date on both the iPad and in iTunes.

2. In iTunes, under the **Apps** tab, you will see **Sync Apps**. It should already be selected. You will also see a mockup of the iPad in iTunes.
3. Select and Deselect the apps you want and don't want to be on the iPad
4. Move the apps around and put them in the order you would like
5. Make folders by dragging one app on top of another. You can also rename the folders
6. Basically get the mockup to look exactly the way you like
7. Sync again. You iPad apps will be in the order and folders you want.

Troubleshooting, an Introduction

For this section, I tried to come up with all of the things that have happened to me with the iPad, as well as others that I have learned about, and the ways in which we have solved those problems. Most problems come down to this: the iPad has been on for so long, you have used it so much and used so many apps that it is just tired and needs to have the power cycled. In other words, reboot. But you will have times where you have a flaky program and it will cause some problems that may require doing a power cycle and/or deleting an app.

How to Deal With Flaky Programs

Here is my logic when it comes to dealing with flaky programs:

1. If I don't really need it, I just delete the program
2. If I like the program or what the program does, I try this:

   - Delete and reinstall

   - If that does not work, I look for alternatives

3. If I love the program, and I can't live without it, I try and contact the developer for support.

I have found some developers to be very open to support issues, but some others are not and don't even return emails. It is a mixed bag. Since these are relatively inexpensive programs, my default thinking is that I will not get much in the way of support. That said, special needs developers will want to hear from you, good and bad, and most of them are incredibly responsive.

 Note: Apple must approve all versions of the software, even minor bug fixes, so it will take time to go from a problem to a solution to approval from Apple to installing the app again on your iPad. I plan for this by having a couple of programs in each category of skill I am looking to develop.

Standby or Off?

You can either choose to turn off your iPad every time and then wait for it to re-start, or you can just leave it in Standby mode. I find that people who think of the iPad as a large cell phone tend to keep it in standby mode and never turn it off. Those who think about it as a mini computer tend to turn it off.

To turn the iPad off and on:

1. Tap and hold the power button for 2-3 seconds until the red **Slide to power off** slider appears.
2. Drag the **Slide to power off** slider to the right to turn off the iPad.
3. To Power up the device, tap and hold the power button long enough to see the white Apple logo appear on screen. The iPad will present you with the lock screen after a minute. Unlock to use.

To put your iPad into and out of Standby mode:

1. Tap on the power button and release, do not hold. This will make the screen turn off and the iPad will be in standby mode.
2. To get out of standby mode, either tap on the home button or tap on the power button or slide the slider above the volume rocker, all three will get you to the lock screen. Unlock to use.

You would, and this is general advice, want to power down if you were traveling in an airport or not going to use the iPad for a long period of time. If you are a frequent user, then you will likely put the iPad into standby mode. We almost never power the devices down unless we have to. Standby mode uses surprisingly little battery life, at least with the wi-fi version.

Power Cycle

When it comes to troubleshooting, the iPad is similar to a lot of other computer devices. Sometimes turning it off and back on again fixes a lot of issues. In other words, power cycle or reboot the iPad.

To power cycle, do the following:

1. Press and hold the power button long enough for the **Slide to Power off** slider to appear
2. Drag the slider to the **off** position. The device will power down all the way, and the screen will go black.
3. Wait at least 10 seconds. This clears the memory. Some will say less, some will say more. The point is, wait before you turn it back on.
4. Press and hold the power button again until you see the Apple logo and then after it boots, the lock screen.

Power cycling works for two main reasons. First, it clears the ram (working memory) of the device. When you use the iPad and are switching back and forth between programs, or are just generally using the iPad, you are loading and unloading a lot of data and programs. Developers try to create rock solid programs, but stuff happens, and it can get a little frazzled in there. By power cycling, you are starting fresh. The second reason is that when you reboot, you are also pulling and loading a clear version of the operating system. When things get frazzled in there and starting going awry, it can effect the base system as well. Pulling and loading a new base system can make everything better in and of itself.

If All Else Fails: Restore and Reset

Technically, there are two actions that are very similar to each other in terms of outcome. They are Restore and Reset.

1. Restore can be done through iTunes. During the Restore process, you will backup the iPad, remove all data from the device, do a fresh installation of the operating system, then you can choose whether or not to add all of your stuff back to your iPad.
2. Reset can be done on an iPad directly in one of two ways: via the **Settings** app or, if the device is not responsive, via a button combination. Resetting will remove all of your data from the iPad. The iPad will use the internally stored operating system to restore a fresh version of the operating system. Unless you use iCloud, your stuff will not be there until you sync with iTunes.

How to Restore the iPad via iTunes

To restore using iTunes, follow these instructions:

1. Plug the iPad into your computer and launch iTunes
2. Select the device and go to the device Summary Page
3. Under the **Version** section, perform a **Restore** on the device.

Screenshot of iTunes Device Summary Page, Restore Button Under Version Section

How to Reset the iPad via General Tab

You can also reset the iPad directly using the **Settings** program on the iPad. There are a number of options. To Reset via the "Settings" app, follow these instructions:

1. Tap on the **Settings** app, **General** tab, tap on **Reset**
2. In the Reset menu, you have a number of options:

   - **Reset All Settings:** This option will NOT delete your content, just your settings.

   - **Erase All Content and Settings:** This option will delete everything on the iPad and bring the device back to the original factory settings

   - **Reset Network Settings:** This only deletes your network settings

- **Reset Keyboard Dictionary:** This only deletes your keyboard dictionary

- **Reset Home Screen Layout:** This will reset the Home screen back to the original version, but will not delete apps

- **Reset Location Warnings:** This will delete the location requests made by apps.

Screenshot of Settings, General, Reset

 Note: Most of the time you will want to use **Erase All content and Settings** for any time you wish to return to the factory reset.

How to Reset the iPad via Buttons

In the event that you are unable to use the software reset options and you would like to reset the iPad, there is a way to do this via the buttons:

1. Press and hold the **Power/Wake** button and then the Home Button for 10 or more seconds until you see the Apple boot icon. Let go of the button.
2. Using this button combination and hold time is the equivalent of **Reset all Set-**

tings and may take anywhere from 10 to 15 minutes to complete.

When to Reset

Why you would choose one reset method over another and what you wish to reset will depend on your circumstances. If, for example, the iPad is not responding at all via software, then a button based reset may be your only option. Always try to do a Restore from iTunes, as this will backup and restore your data. But whatever it is you have to do, make sure to sync regularly and you will be OK no matter what.

Only once have I had to do any kind of reset on the device. Typically power cycling will resolve most of your issues.

The Dreaded Jiggles

The dreaded jiggles is a common new user issue only because there is not really anything comparable to it in other devices. Once you understand what it is and how to deal with it, it is easy to recognize. Here is what will happen - you will do something, not really realizing what you did, and then all of the sudden the app icons will start to jiggle. Then you will ask yourself, "Why are all the app icons on my home screen jiggling and what does the 'X' in the black circle in the upper left hand corner of the app mean?" The next question will likely be, "How do I make it stop?" This same issue could also be presented to you as, "What happened to all of the apps on my home screen?"

The dreaded jiggles are a by-product of tapping and holding on an app icon for an extended period of time, say 2-3 seconds. It is analogous in the computer world to a right mouse click. When you are on the home screen, you put your finger on an app and hold for 2-3 second, the icon will jiggle and an "X" in a black circle will appear. If you were to tap on the "X" in the black circle, you would erase the app from the iPad. You can get it back by "buying" and downloading it again. Not to worry, you will not pay for it twice - as long as it is the exact same app and you are using the exact same Apple ID account.

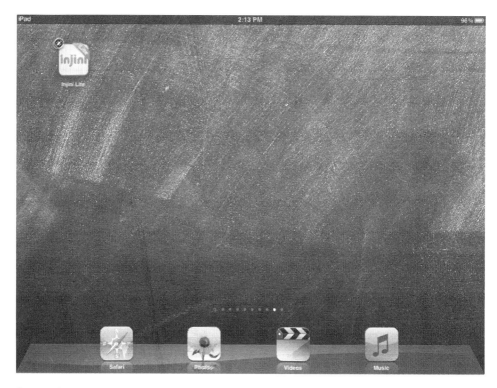

Screenshot App Jiggles

As you can imagine, erasing apps can be fun for some users and you could find that within no time at all that every app on your iPad has been erased. Joy. There are two aspects to solving this problem:

Step 1: Are any apps missing? If not move to step 2, if so:

1. If it is one or two apps and you know what they are, you can go into the App Store on the iPad under purchased and re-download them
2. If there are a number of apps missing and or you don't remember what you had, plug the iPad into your computer with iTunes and Sync. This will restore all of the apps from the last sync.

Step2: Prevent apps from being deleted in the first place:

1. Under **Settings**, **General**, tap on **Restrictions**.
2. Tap **Enable Restrictions** and pick a pin number. Write it down and keep it in a safe place. My kids are young, so I used a label-maker and put the pin on the back of each of the iPads. Since they are inside of the case, my kids don't know

it is there. This will not work for long.

3. Once Restrictions are enabled, tap the **Deleting Apps** slider from On (default) to Off. No more jiggles.

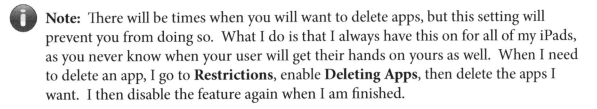 **Note:** There will be times when you will want to delete apps, but this setting will prevent you from doing so. What I do is that I always have this on for all of my iPads, as you never know when your user will get their hands on yours as well. When I need to delete an app, I go to **Restrictions**, enable **Deleting Apps**, then delete the apps I want. I then disable the feature again when I am finished.

Music Coming From the iPad Even When It Is Off

Sometimes it will seem like a ghost has gotten hold of the iPad and there is music playing from it, even when it is turned off. First, there are ghosts, and believe me, your iPad has been possessed. Just kidding. There is a simple explanation: the iPad evolved from the iPod, which is first and foremost a portable music player, so it has the ability to play music and simultaneously play apps or have the screen turned off. We don't generally think of the iPad as being a multitasking device able to do two

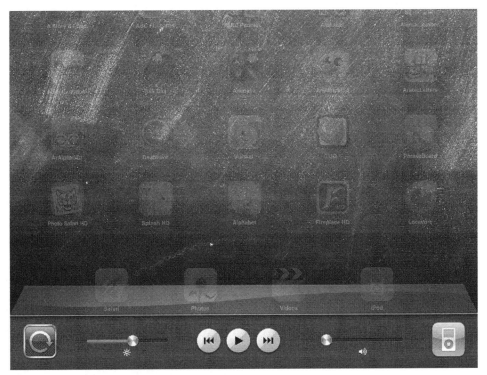

Screenshot of the Multitasking User Interface

things at once, since most of the time we only do one at a time, and in most cases, you can only do one thing at a time with the iPad. So when you hear music unexpectedly, it is counter-intuitive to your general experience with the iPad.

Here is the long way to address it:

1. Tap the Home or Power button
2. Unlock the screen
3. Double tap on the Home button, which will launch the Multitasking User Interface
4. Swipe to the right to reveal the Rotation Lock/Mute Lock button, brightness and contrast and the music app area. Right in the middle of the screen you will find the music controls. While you are hearing music, the play button will be on. Tap it to pause and stop the music.
5. Double tap the Home button to return to the Home screen

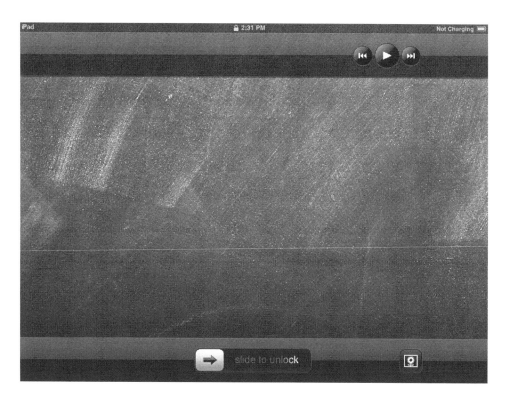

Screenshot of Lock Screen with Music Controls

Here is the shortcut:

1. If the iPad screen is off but you hear music, double tap the Home button. This will launch the lock screen with music controls.
2. Use the music controls to turn off the music or, if you desire, skip to the previous or next song.

Icons Not Rotating

Every once in a while you will use the iPad long enough that the icons on the Home screen will stop rotating. When it happens, and you will know it if and when it does, the screen goes from portrait (4 icons across and 5 icon rows down) to landscape (5 icons across and 4 rows down), but the icons don't rotate and the columns don't change. The icons are cut off and it just looks like something is going wrong.

What do you do:

1. Power cycle the iPad and everything should go back to normal.
2. If that fails, then perform a Reset.
3. If that fails, take it to Apple.

 Note: This has happened to me about 6 or so times so far, and a power cycle is all that has been needed.

Sounds Funny

A lot of the iPad apps have catchy little tunes. After hearing them over and over and over so many times, you might hope they would just fade away, but every once and a while, the app just sounds funny. You will know it when it happens, the music has an echo, or it double plays or an effect plays, but the sound track does not when it should.

What do you do:

1. Power cycle the iPad, everything should go back to normal.
2. If that fails, then perform a Reset.
3. If that fails, take it to Apple.

Note: I have never had to do anything but power cycle to take care of this problem

 Note: This problem emerges more often after a major operating system update.

No Sound

There are a number of settings that affect the sound output of the iPad. A simple example is the Mute/UnMute button. Most of the time when you think there should be sound and there is not, you or someone else has inadvertently changed some of the settings. Here is how I go about troubleshooting sound problems:

1. Is Mute turned on? Check the slider to see if it is set to mute and check the Multitask Bar (double tap on the Home button, swipe to the right to reveal the preference area).
2. Determine if you can hear any sound at all or absolutely none. Check the Video, Music, and Alerts. If you can hear sound from some and not from others, it is most likely a settings issue. Determine what you cannot hear and go to the settings for that item to see if the sound is turned off.
3. If there is no sound anywhere and you are really perplexed, try a hard boot. Press and hold the home and power buttons for more than 10 seconds until you get the white Apple logo.
4. If this does not fix it, then perform an iTunes reset.

Did My iPad Just Die?

"I know the iPad is charged but it just will not turn on." This really happened to me. We called it the Black Screen of Death. I tried everything I could think of, and then thought to myself, "Here we go, it is broken and we have only had it for a few months. What am I going to do?" I went to the Apple store and that is where I learned about the button reset. They did it for me and all was well, the iPad came back to life about 10 minutes after the reset with all of my data intact. To perform a button reset:

1. Press and hold the **Power/Wake** button and the Home button for 10 seconds or longer, until the Apple icon appears on screen.
2. The reset process may take 10-15 minutes.

Note: Of course, if this does not work you will need to have a professional look at your iPad.

The Screen Is Cracked!

This also happened to me, on a relatively new iPad2. It was in my bag and for some reason, the screen cracked. Here is what you do:

1. Determine if the problem is more than the screen. Try and turn it on.
2. If the iPad turns on, then you can have the screen replaced by a service: Apple, local phone repair place, mail order service
3. If it does not turn on, you will have to decide:

   - Do I want to fix it?

   - Can it be fixed and for how much?

   - You will need to have someone look at it: Apple store, local phone repair place, send it off.

When this happened to me, I went to a local iPhone/iPad repair store. They looked at it and noted it could still be turned on, so they replaced the screen. It was expensive, but still much less than a new iPad. If it had been more than just the screen repair, it would likely not have been worth fixing.

 Note: using anyone other than the Apple store for this sort of repair may get your iPad back into full operating condition, but it may also void your warranty on the product.

Will Not Keep a Charge

This problem happened to me with an iPod Touch. We had it for a while and it worked and charged fine. Then for no apparent reason, it stopped holding a charge. Every time we charged it, it would charge fine and show a full battery, but after 30 minutes off the charger, it would be dead. I thought the battery was dying or dead. It seem logical, but I called Apple and the person instructed me to do the following:

1. Plug the iPod into your computer and launch iTunes
2. Select the device and go to the device summary page

3. Under the "Version" section, perform a Restore on the device.

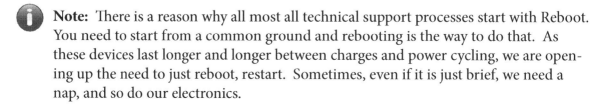

Screenshot of iPad Summary Screen in iTunes showing restore button.

Note: After performing a restore, the iPod charged and held a charge just fine and still does. It is counter-intuitive that this would work, but I think this experience can be applied to a number of bad device behaviors.

Not Quite Right

This is the catch all section, when you are looking at the iPad and it is looking back at you a little wonky. You will know it is just not quite right; here is what you do:

1. Power Cycle.

Note: There is a reason why all most all technical support processes start with Reboot. You need to start from a common ground and rebooting is the way to do that. As these devices last longer and longer between charges and power cycling, we are opening up the need to just reboot, restart. Sometimes, even if it is just brief, we need a nap, and so do our electronics.

Index

Thank You

22395535R00180

Made in the USA
Lexington, KY
26 April 2013